The BOOK *of* CLIFFORD

CLIFFORD PARKER

PAGE PUBLISHING, INC.
New York, NY

First originally published by Page Publishing, Inc. 2019

ISBN 978-1-64462-012-0 (Paperback)
ISBN 978-1-64462-013-7 (Digital)

Printed in the United States of America

A Cricket in the Wrong Place

"There is a difference." Because I am a cautious person you will need to read between the lines. If you are easily offended, you may not want to read this story. I'm going to discuss the facts of life. No, not *those* facts but something very similar. Have you ever seen that cartoon where two little kids are shown standing side by side and they are staring down into their underwear? The caption under the picture says, "There is a difference?" Well, that's a fact of life and yes, we guys are different from our female counterparts. Not just physically but numerous other ways too!

My son and I are outnumbered by the women in our lives. We work in an office full of women, and our personal lives are outnumbered by more women. We don't have a chance.

This setup has allowed the two of us to probably hear more things about women than we really want to know, but I must say that hearing a lot of these things have been well for me in my understanding of women. I just hope my son catches on to these things as well as I have.

I have learned a whole lot about the ups and downs of each month, the process and issues surrounding childbirth, and yes, even the special names given to various areas. Men have always done this, but women do too. (Okay, ladies, admit it. You know you and your lady friends have laughed and made jokes about the anatomy just like men do.)

3

If any of you have watched the TV show *Everybody Loves Raymond*, you know that Ray has talked about his special names for special areas. I have seen other shows that advertise women's clothes, and they even use slang terms for areas too. I guess for that matter, there was a recent article in a newspaper I just read today that a judge in another state has stopped a local school district from requiring the students to remove some bracelets. It seems there is a big push right now with a program that states, "I love boobies." (Don't get upset at me for using this word. It's all over the place.) It is a cancer awareness program, and the kids have been wearing these bracelets with this wording. The school district thought it was inappropriate, and they had the kids remove them, so somebody sued. The judge agreed with the kids, and now they are wearing these in school. Now if you think about it, where did that name come from? Why do we need to rename parts that already have names? Doesn't this just cause confusion? Too many names for one single area. What if people don't speak the same language and they get the areas confused? (Now I can already hear some of you rattling off the various names you have heard. Admit it. You are doing this in your mind right now.)

Well, this leads me to the next part of this story. In order to protect the innocent, I will not disclose full names.

There is a guy named Mike who recently had a really bad day. It started out when a brand-new tire on his truck started going flat first thing in the morning. That's always a bad sign when your day starts out with a flat or a car that won't start. He tried airing the tire up, but it kept leaking. His lug wrench was missing, so he had to call a friend who helped him change his tire. He threw the leaking tire in the bed of his truck, and during the morning, while the truck sat out front, they heard an explosion inside the building. The tire had bubbled up and blew out the sidewall. So much for a bad day.

It seemed like the next day was no better. Mike was making his way down a busy road when suddenly, he felt something in his pants. He was in a panic as this crawly thing moved from the waist-band area, down his side, and headed between his legs and around and around in his pants. In a panic, he began to pull his truck to the side of the road. He bailed out of his truck, jumped around like a madman, undid his pants, grabbed at his waistband, and pulled it away, staring into his drawers to see what was going on down there as a cricket jumped from his underwear to freedom. I'm sure some people who saw him thought he was trying to find something that he thought he had lost. If you saw him, just know that Mike is not crazy, and he is just fine. Just trying to protect what little—never mind.

A Joke Gone Bad

"Art, Art, Where are you Art? Art, come in here right now! Art, are you listening to me? Where are you, Art?" The sounds of Marylin—I can still hear them ringing in my ears after all these years.

Art and Marylin Cummings have been family friends for many, many years. Art and I went to high school together, and after a few years, we settled into the same church.

After my wife and I were married, we joined a church known as Grace Tabernacle in Tomball, Texas. Art and Marylin were married and joined the same church. We both have daughters about the same age.

Art and Marylin used to live in a mobile home parked behind the church. As time passed, our families grew close, and we began to tease each other about the ways in which each of us treated our spouses. Art and Marylin took the brunt of most jokes because we accused Art of being henpecked. Marylin had a way of calling out to Art from inside the house. Her voice would hit nasal octaves, which could be heard reverberating between the church building and metal walls of the house for hundreds of yards away. Regardless of where Art was on the church property, he would always promptly respond with his typical "Yes, honey," and then go off and do whatever he wanted to do in the first place. Most of us men respond with the same answer. We always tell our wives what they want to hear but do it our own way anyhow.

Marylin was one to always be involved in a good joke. She could dish them out, but she could take them as well. One day a joke was played that went real bad.

A workday was being held at the church. As with most of us, we are happy to help when we can. I had been at the church for several hours and was soon ready to leave. I had no desire to go announce to everyone I was leaving because I knew I would get picked on for being the first one to leave, so I simply left. I didn't tell a soul I was leaving.

As I drove up the driveway at home, my wife came running out the door screaming at me to get back up to the church because Marylin called and said the church house was on fire! As I turned to run back to my car, I told her to call the fire department.

I had been a volunteer fireman for several years, and I knew the drill as I was making my way back to town. A call would go in to the dispatcher at the police department, and a siren would sound off at Bill Snyder's old house on East Main. I knew if I drove with my window down, I would be able to hear the alarm as it was being rung and would need to watch out for the trucks as they pulled out of the station. The closer I got to town, the more and more my ears strained to hear the sounds of the alarms.

As I began approaching the church house from Main, I strained to see the smoke. I really anticipated seeing black smoke billowing from all angles of the church when a little voice inside my head told me to hold back and not rush to the scene without a moment of caution. I turned one block early and circled the church house from a one-block distance. I soon saw the fire truck parked in front of the church, but the hoses were dry and still lying on the truck. The sirens were not on, and I failed to see anybody scurrying around in much of a hurry.

That small voice started telling me somebody was pulling my leg. After circling the block a couple of times, I soon garnered the courage to drive into the lot. As I got out of my car, I realized a prank that was attempting to be pulled on me had turned real sour.

What really occurred was the fact Marylin had called my home, attempting to force me to rush back to the church since I left workday without telling anyone. What she failed to tell my wife was this was in fact a joke, so when I got home and my wife told me the church was on fire, I immediately told her to call the fire department. My wife then started calling other church members, and soon everybody in church was panicking, thinking the church was burning down.

For once I was innocent and this prank turned bad by causing the volunteer firemen to come out and creating a lot of potential problems.

Art and Marylin have moved, and the church has changed names. Life goes on, and my memories of Art and Marylin will be forever.

Art and Marilyn

ARE YOU WILLING TO SACRIFICE?

Many of you know me as a happy-go-lucky kind of fellow. I enjoy life and can usually find humor in most things. I want to change hats today and ask you some questions from the heart. Many of you may find this as an editorial, so if that's the way you read it, then just remember that none of the words in this article are anyone's thoughts but my own. They do not reflect the thoughts or ideas of my family or anyone else but me.

I have been catching, off and on, bits and pieces of various civil war stories that are circulating on TV. I have watched some of these stories in absolute awe of the personal sacrifices some of these families have given to birth this nation during those days. I know that the ultimate sacrifice is the human lives that were lost. I understand this, and if I could, I would tell these people that I appreciate what they did for this country. But the truth is, their sacrifice is final and it's over. I am not and would not belittle the sacrifice of human life, and that is not what this story is about. I want to focus on the other side of the picture, and that is the sacrifice of those who are living.

First of all, the worst sadness in living is burying a loved one. Regardless of the relationship with a loved one, the death of that person leaves a hole in the heart of the living. Each and every day, we can have a thought about them and that spot of sadness can remain with us forever. Think of this country and the families that have given their loved ones and the sadness that still remains but, but when it's all said and done, the percentage of population that has lost a loved one in war in current society is very small in comparison to those who benefit from that sacrifice. Again, I will always hold anyone who serves this country in a higher esteem, but again, those who serve are small in number in comparison to those they protect.

I was born in 1952 and was slated for draft during the Vietnam era. The lottery system was in place, and I was number five on the lottery and carried a 1A classification. I knew I was headed to service, but when I was called up for my physical, they classified me as 4F. Was I scared when they called me up? Of course, I was. Was I relieved when I was told I was physically disqualified? Sure. But as I look back now, I tend to realize a small part of life passed me by because I feel somewhat guilty because I have never had to sacrifice for my country. I have seen the effects of war through the eyes of the media, but I will say that as a citizen of this country, I have never really had to sacrifice for the wars I have seen. The same applies for this country as a whole. The former generations that had to give personal sacrifice are now in the minority.

Have you ever had an opposing army come into your home and confiscate your personal belongings away and burn your home? Have you ever heard canons firing near the edge of your town or community and you had to grab a few belongings and abandon your home? Have any of us ever had to stand in line to obtain our ration of food or water? I am sure the generation before me can remember the sacrifices of World War II, but were your sacrifices really that deep? Did you really sacrifice anything other than creature comforts? Did an opposing army stop by your home and confiscate things?

Once again, I am not talking about the human suffering of giving of one's life or family member to our country. There is no comparison, but what about the rest of us? I cannot remember ever having to sacrifice for any war in my lifetime. What about the next generation? Will war become so sanitized that it will be just another news story that we will see and then go on about our lives with the minority numbers of people handling our problems?

What have we gained in this country by these wars that do not require sacrifice of its majority? Have we increased the size of our land mass? Have we increased our Christian influence and values across the world? Have we held back the growth and influence of government in our lives? Have we, the people, obtained any tangible benefits from our lack of sacrifice, or could the opposite be true maybe? Has our lack of personal sacrifice caused us to no longer be willing to complete the jobs we started, or will we always go halfway in our battles and then quit? Have our Christian values actually been diminished in this world? Has the government grown and required more of our lives than before? Have we really seen any tangible benefits?

Some would argue that we have in fact benefited. We have not had shots fired on US soil. Our lifestyle in America is still high. Our ability to produce and import and export is still high, so some would say the wars of my lifetime have been very beneficial. Really? So have we now moved into an era of foregoing the things this country was founded on such as Christian values, less government, and freedom into an era of no sacrifice, more government, and less freedoms? Has our personal lack of sacrifice for this country moved us from holding high the standards of heartfelt, human values and replacing them with comfort values instead? Are we more moral today than we were when war required sacrifice? Do we have more freedoms and less government? Seems to me quite the opposite is true, and looks to me like the enemy has made their way into our homes and we don't even know it because we have chosen comfort over sacrifice.

Maybe what this country needs is a wake-up call of sacrifice. I think we have all fallen asleep at the wheel and allowed ourselves to be rocked into a deep slumber of nonsacrifice because we have become comfortable. I have a personal feeling that we will soon be awakened. I personally feel that sacrifice is on the way. I just hope we can all be ready.

BASEBALL PLAYERS

Well, spring has sprung, and there is love in the air. The reason I know love is in the air is because of two incidents that occurred this past weekend. I hope I can put them into words, and I hope this doesn't become one of those stories where you have to be there to appreciate the humor of the moment.

I drove to Independence, Texas, one Saturday to check on Leon. Leon was one of my past therapists I use who hears all my frustrations. He listens very intently, and he only charges me a sack of feed or a bale of hay every once in a while. As I arrived at the ranch, I allowed Leon and all the ladies grazing access to our yard area for a few hours. As time passed, I soon heard Leon standing next to the neighbor's fence line, letting out some of those low guttural moaning and bellows to his neighbor next door. The kind of deep-gutted, throaty, low bellows that says to the neighbor, "I'm stronger than you, and I'm gonna whip you if you even think of lookin' at my ladies over here." The kind of bellow that says, "I'm gonna beat you up if you set one foot on my land."

After about an hour of exchanges of grunts and calls between each other, Leon's neighbor sauntered up to the fence to exchange some close-up words. The grunting became louder and louder, and soon they got into the dirt-kickin' stage. A good bull can dig a hole a couple of feet deep and several feet wide if the ground is soft enough, and between the two of them, eventually they will have a hole dug under the fence big enough to drive a Mack truck under it. I decided it was time to separate these two before they started jostling the fence back and forth, and I was eventually able to force Leon back into the main pasture. Leon had love on his mind.

When I left the ranch, I decided to stop in Brenham, Texas, and have lunch. There used to be a real good restaurant in Brenham called Purcell's. They served an excellent buffet of all kinds of meats and vegetables and a good dessert bar. I always left mad. Mad because I always ate too much. Sadly, they closed a few years ago.

I enjoy watching people. My people watching inspire many of my thoughts and ideas for my stories. I watch somebody do something really funny, and it will remind me of times in my own life when similar things have occurred.

As I was enjoying my lunch and watching people, I noticed two women enter the premises. By the way they were dressed (undressed would be a better description), it became very obvious to me these two women were not part of the local Chamber of Commerce or Welcome Wagon. These were the kind of women who—I mean they appeared to—they looked like, well, you just had to be there to understand what I mean. (Yes, I have already told my wife this story.)

An elderly man and his wife were sitting across from me. This guy first looked at the two women, turned his head away, glanced back at them again, turned his head, and looked back a third time, always checking to see if his wife was looking at his eyes wandering off in the distance. It would have really been funny if he would have taken off his glasses to clean them, but he didn't.

The next guy I observed was a wandering kind of fella. He would wander around and around the food bar acting like he was looking at the food, when in reality I saw his eyes always following each and every move these women made. I'll bet he checked out the entire food service area at least four times before he ever picked up the first kernel of corn. He appeared to load his plate one pea at a time, always having a reason to go back for another look.

The next group of guys, however, took the prize. A group of high school baseball players were in the restaurant. They were from Carroll High School in the Corpus Christie, Texas, area. One of the players rounded the dessert bar and stopped in his tracks, almost falling backward when walking into the sight of these two women. A big grin came over his face as he hurriedly moved back to his side of the restaurant. I knew right away what this kid was about to do. He felt it his manly obligation to go share the vision he just had with all his buddies, and sure nough, about thirty seconds later, at least half the players were suddenly in the mood for some more desserts. These guys rushed the dessert bar like buzzards on a dead cow. So many of the fellas headed toward the dessert bar that I almost jumped up to get my own desert, thinking they were going to wipe it out, when I suddenly realized they weren't actually getting any desserts. They were simply circling the bar time and time again to get another look at these women.

After a few minutes, the two women finally got their plates filled with food and made their way to their booth.

I kept laughing to myself at the obvious activities these guys had just involved themselves in. All of them suddenly, simultaneously, and with one accord had a dessert craving while I knew all along what they were actually up to. They were simply trying to get their eyes full and could care less about the food at the time.

After a few minutes and probably a lot of bantering, betting, elbowing, daring, and harassing each other, one guy who appeared the be the biggest of the group stood up from the table. I watched him wander the long way around several tables and finally approach these two women from the backside of a booth. I'm sure the whole time he was trying to get up his nerve to speak to these two women who were several years his senior. I watched him slide himself into the booth behind them and lean around the end of the booth and begin talking to these two women. One of them ignored him, and the other one simply got a grin on her face like she had been there and done that before. I really think she simply wanted to give this young man his moment of glory in front of his buddies, so she listened to what he had to say. I know he spoke to them for at least a good sixty seconds, and then proudly got up and walked away in that bantam rooster walk we guys get when we think we have risen above a small mountain when talking to the opposite sex.

I told you love is in the air. Two incidents in one day, and the spring flowers are about to bloom. The passions of bulls and young men grow stronger and stronger every day.

BULLHEADED BOYS:
JASON, GLEN, AND ROGER

I went to the ranch one day to check on my cows. It was so dry at the ranch that when I slapped a mosquito on my arm, he dropped his canteen. I even saw a dog standing near a fire hydrant, and the hydrant was trying to bribe the dog. Okay, okay, I know you have heard those before—dumb jokes. I just couldn't help myself, sorry.

Most of us guys are pretty dumb sometimes. We laugh at dumb jokes and do dumb things especially when we are young. I guess as we begin to age, we develop a real understanding that our parents weren't so dumb after all. I don't care how many times a young man is told not to do something. He's going to do it anyway just because he was told not to do it.

As I was driving my tractor around the fence row, it made me think of two of my nephews named Jason and Glen. I drove past a piece of fence one of them helped me repair many years ago, and seeing the fence repair brought these stories back to my recollection.

Several years ago, I took Jason up to the ranch for a day's work. Jason was probably twelve or thirteen years old at the time.

I was using a cutting torch to cut some metal, and for some reason, I also was using one of those cheap paring knives in my work. It's one of those little seventy-nine-cent knives with a plastic handle and a flimsy blade. I must have been using it to scrape a mark in the metal or something.

17

As I finished making a cut along one piece of metal, I turned to Jason and asked him to hold the cutting torch so I wouldn't have to relight it as I repositioned my metalwork. I also handed him the paring knife. My last instruction to him was very explicit. I said, "Jason, don't pass that flame near anything. It is extremely hot and will burn anything that it touches in a split second. Do you understand me, son?" His immediate reply was, "Yes, sir." I turned away from him to move my work, and within ten or fifteen seconds, I turned back his way and there was this pitiful image of a young, teenage boy with a hangdog look. In one hand he held my cutting torch, and in the other hand he held a piece of curled up metal which looked like a pig's tail all melted into the handle of what was once a paring knife. I looked straight at him and asked him why he had passed the torch over the knife, and his answer was, "To see if it was really hot." Okay, he was educated that it was hot, he saw it was hot because he saw it melt metal, and he could feel it was hot. So what's the problem? It's all because I told him.

A few weeks later, I took his brother Glen with me for another weekend of work. As Glen and I were working along the back fence line making repairs, I asked Glen to climb though the barbed wire and work with me from the other side of the fence. During his young teenage years, Glen would occasionally wear some of those baggy pants. Kind of like the bell-bottoms I used to wear in the seventies except his leg bottoms were the size of a circus tent. As we had finished our repairs to the fence, I told him he could crawl back through the fence as we were ready to call it a day. He perched himself on top of an old log and said, "Uncle Clifford, watch this."

I could tell he was going to try to jump this barbed wire fence. I stopped him and said, "Glen, don't do that! That fence is higher than it seems to you, son, and you don't want to get tangled up in that wire!"

I turned my back to him to pick up some tools when, all of a sudden, I heard a familiar sound of barbed wire fence being stretched under pressure. I swung my head around to find Glen with his back on the ground and one leg wrapped between two of the tightly stretched gaucho fence wires we had just strung. I asked him why he jumped after I had very plainly told him not to, and his only remark was, "I thought I could make it."

Not only do we guys do dumb things, but we also have quirky, funny things we do as kids. Makes me think of Roger, the younger brother to Jason and Glen. I can remember that when he was a youngster his mom would have a birthday party for him. As the candles were lit, we all stood around singing Happy Birthday to Roger and he would start crying. For some reason, singing Happy Birthday to him made him cry. It got to the point after three or four years in a row that my son and I enjoyed singing to him just to see him cry. As much as everybody tried to teach him that the birthday song was supposed to make him happy, he continued to cry and get mad.

I don't understand why we guys don't listen. As little boys, we failed to listen to our parents. As teenagers we failed to listen to our parents and as husbands we fail to listen to our wife and parents. We just don't listen to anybody. (Oh boy, I'm in trouble now. I just ratted on myself.)

Three Little Farts

CABBAGE LEAVES FOR WHAT?

This story is for men only. If you are a female reader, I urge you to put this story down right now and walk away. I am taking a great leap this week, and I am sneaking this story to the paper unseen and unedited by my wife. I have always had a deal with her that I would never write a story that she has not read. If I start making women mad, I get into trouble from all sides. My wife, my in-laws, my aunts, my cousins, my daughter, and all the women in my office are apt to get me into a lot of trouble. The reason they all edit my stories is so I can continue walking the streets of town without someone throwing eggs on me. My wife informs me that sometimes the things I think are funny can be offensive to others. She also continues to warn me that we men have a sick sense of humor and many women would find my manly thought process way out of line, so her duty is to keep me on the straight and narrow. I am straying from the proper path this week and am sneaking this story in the paper with an announcement to all men. Eve didn't wear fig leaves. I have it from a very good source that she probably actually wore cabbage leaves and not fig leaves. Please let me explain.

Ever since I was a little boy, the women in my life have been trying to keep me on the right path. How many times did your mom tell you to make sure you had clean underwear with no holes in them in case you were involved in a car accident? How many times did you get into trouble for getting mud all over yourself? Has your wife ever complained because you had dirty fingernails or grease on your hands? Has she ever told you how rough the calluses on your hands were? These are all very manly attributes of ourselves. What's wrong with all these very natural things that happen to us men? Who are the women of our lives to think that they can continue to control us all the time, when the truth is women are the ones who are really nuts! Consider the fact that dirt, grease, holey underwear, passing gas, and callused hands are all very natural occurrences. On the flip side, however, have any of you men ever considered what our womenfolk are doing to themselves? They take mud and smear it on their bodies and call it a mud bath. It's a beauty aid. They use aloe plants for their hands and also use a hand lotion called udder balm. They are washing their hair in all sorts of fruits. They use shampoo designed for horses. They use potatoes to poke holes in their earlobes. (I know, I know, some men are doing this too.) Women place potatoes or fruits on their eyes to sooth them, and now for the big kicker, they are using cabbage leaves to relieve the pain associated with new mothers who are producing milk. No kidding, men! I have now learned that women who have just given birth are placing cabbage leaves on their…well, on their…well, you know. They are using cabbage to help take away the pains associated with their milk production! Can you imagine that? What if we men started placing mustard greens on our special part to ease the personal manly drives we have? Do you get my drift? Have you ever heard women tell a man to go take a cold shower? Can you imagine your wife telling you to go place a pile of mustard greens on yourself to relieve your sudden urges? What if she said, "Not tonight, honey, go get some pineapple slices and place them down there." What if watermelon worked? Can you imagine the run on watermelons we men would have once they are in season? I can read the headlines now: "As the first load of watermelons hit our stores today, a man was trampled at the watermelon stand as the crowd of men rushed the counter for their first watermelon of the season."

I guess I'm in enough trouble now, so I better stop, but I'm sure now that Adam and Eve wore cabbage leaves instead of fig leaves because if they wore fig leaves, they would have probably shriveled up like a prune.

The Un-Named Lady

CHEAP FUN

I really do believe that a group of private citizens can do a better job of budgeting this country than most of the people we have serving in Washington. Number one, I don't think many of them have any idea what the real money looks like, and number two, even if they did, they would think money grows on trees. Maybe what should be done is real green money needs to be placed throughout the rooms where they meet and make them split the green cash money into budget items just like we used to do in grade school with change. This concept gives you a better handle on how soon you can run out of money instead of just playing with the numbers on papers. Okay, okay, I'm through complaining now, and the above comments were my own and they are nobody else's but my own. Don't blame my family for what I think.

I do, however, want to help you today with some real money-saving ideas when it comes to entertainment. Now most men will probably try this at some point in their life, but I doubt many women would take these refreshing, free entertainment ideas to heart. I can assure you these are great ways to have fun, and yes, I have in fact done these things before.

Most people don't like those phone solicitation calls. I, on the other hand, see them as opportunities. Opportunities to have fun. This could be some of the ways to try this new idea. *Ring, ring.*

"Hello."

"Can I speak to Mr. Parker?"

"This is him, sweetheart," I would say in my skillfully disguised old man's voice.

"Mr. Parker, I would like to talk to you about your satellite system you have in your new car."

"Honey, I don't have a new car."

"Oh, well, is there another Mr. Parker in your home?"

"Yes, honey, you must be talking about my son. He's outside right now chasing after the neighborhood kids. He caught them trying to steal the corn he put out for the hogs, and he's bound and determined to set a trap and catch them."

"Catch what, Mr. Parker, the hogs?"

"No, honey, the kids! He's tired of them messing around our house, so he's gonna trap them. Listen, sweetheart, you mentioned something about his new car. Now what's wrong with it?"

"Oh, sir, there is nothing wrong with his car, but we wanted to renew his satellite system he has. The free option has expired, and we wanted to help him renew it."

"What do you mean he has a satellite in his car? Aren't those things pretty big? How in the world did they fit a satellite in his car? I haven't seen it, and I've been in his car a few times."

"Oh no, sir, it's not in his car. It helps him navigate his vehicle around town."

"Honey, my son has been driving many years, and I don't think he needs any help driving. He's never had a wreck that I know of. Now, on the other hand, I may need to use it 'cause my driving has gotten pretty bad. I just ran over a guy last week, but I didn't want to stop 'cause that dance show was about to come on television, and I don't ever miss that dance show, no, sirree!"

"Sir, did you say you ran over somebody?"

"No, I didn't run over him. I just hit him a little, and he was okay 'cause he was hit on the dirt in the ditch and not on the hard pavement. Did you want me to go get my son?"

They hung up.

Other ways to have free fun is to go shopping with your wife and sit outside the store in a relaxing position. As people walk by your car, hit the panic button on the horn and watch people jump.

The really funny ones are people who have the phone stuck in the ear while not paying attention to where they are walking. They jump the highest.

Last but not least, place your broken chairs, TVs, water hoses, shovels, anything on the side of the road and see how long it takes somebody to pick it up. This works best on weekends, and the items must always be made to look like they fell off your truck. Don't sit a chair upright. It must be lying on its side with the broken leg pointed toward the ditch. Most people will grab things in a hurry and don't pay attention that the leg just fell off into the grass while they were picking it up. The bigger the item, the funnier this becomes. Sometimes you will see people drive by the items real slow, scouting out the area. They will turn around and drive back by a couple of times. I have even seen people drive by and show back up minutes later with help. I once placed an old table saw on the side of the road and watched four guys jump out of the truck to grab it as if they had just found gold. What they didn't realize is the motor was burned out and the table was warped and the guides were cracked. I think it was an old saw I once picked up myself from the side of the road.

They always say, "What comes around goes around," or maybe it is "What goes around comes around." Hmmm. Oh well. Go have some free entertainment.

Code Names Bruce, Brian, and Blake

I have never met a group of siblings that at some point in their life didn't fight, tussle, or wrestle around. For some reason, we all did that. I don't know why, but it's just born into us. Every generation I have known, at some point in life, have had minor to major disputes.

My brother and sisters and I were no different. We have never and will never have a major knockdown drag out nor have we ever really gotten mad at each other as kids or adults that I can recall. I really don't even remember arguing with them about much of anything, and I never remember wrestling or even punching my sisters on the arm, but for some reason, I recall my brother and I seemed to go through a period of time that we "wrassled." Now if you watch television, those guys wrestle, but my brother and I wrassled. Wrasslin' is what we called it all our lives.

The best I can recall, my brother and I would seem to get into some kind of wrasslin' match immediately after church every Sunday. We went from being forgiven by the Lord, and within thirty minutes, we were already sinnin' again.

I don't know what caused this, but I can remember going to church all dressed up in our little coat and tie and then coming home and get into a wrasslin' match. We wore a nice pair of slacks with a white shirt, tie, and coat. Somehow and someway, the first thing that came off when we got home was the shoes first and then the pants.

I can remember my brother and me rolling around on the bed and floor of our bedroom in a wrasslin' match with our tie, shirt, coat, socks, and white Fruit of the Loom briefs. I have no idea why we fought, and it was probably simply because we knew that the other was very vulnerable about the time a guy gets his pants around his ankles and he can very easily be toppled over when he is all tangled up in his pants. I know this probably did not go on very long, but it seemed like it happened every Sunday.

Of course when Daddy would hear us laughing and the crashes hitting our hardwood floors of the house, he would come in and do his fatherly thing by giving us a whuppin'. He had to do this for several reasons. Number one, the clothes we had just taken off were still clean enough for another Sunday's wear and of course by the time we got through tramplin' the pants and wrinklin' the coat, shirt, and tie, Mamma would have to clean them all over again. Our clothes didn't go to the cleaners all the time like we do nowadays. She washed and actually ironed our clothes, and she already had plenty to do each week without us two boys messin' them up unnecessarily.

Our spankings were always with a belt, and they were administered in the merry-go-round style of spankings. I think someday soon I am going to write a story about the different spanking styles that I know are available. Maybe I can write a parenting book for the younger generation. They seemed to have forgotten the benefits of this educational tool for parenting.

Another group of guys I know that used to fight lived on the other side of town from us. In order to shade their identity, I may use fake names like Bruce, Brian, and Blake. They were a family of three brothers. One of them informed me that he remembers that they used to really, really fight real fights and not just wrasslin' matches. One of them, who I code-named Bruce, told me that his brother Brian was the one who always got everybody into trouble. I guess he was the lead instigator, and Blake and Bruce were the little angels.

Bruce told me a story that as a young boy, he used to plant a garden every year. He enjoyed his garden, and he usually enjoyed doing the work all by himself. He remembered one time when his brother Brian was throwing rocks at him while he was working his garden one summer. He said several of the rocks made connection, and they did in fact hurt, but the rock throwing was more of a nuisance than actual pain. Suddenly when one of the rocks made connection on Bruce's body, he remembers falling to the ground and screaming and yelling and crying out in fake pain. It was mostly to get Brian in trouble, and so Bruce was really putting on a great show in case his mom or dad may have seen the deed done by Brian.

As he lay in the middle of his garden for an extended period of time, putting on a great show to get Brian into the best trouble he could, the neighbor suddenly came running across the field, thinking he was is such great distress that he was about to meet with the real angels in heaven.

Bruce is still embarrassed to this day that the neighbor thought he needed real help and it was all for show that happened over fifty years ago.

The thing about family however is this. While we all tussled, fought, and wrestled around as siblings, don't anybody ever step between any of us and our family. If you mess with our families, you won't know what trouble is until you mess with somebody's sibling. We can tussle around all we want, but you better not butt in 'cause you ain't seen nothin' when you mess with somebody's family.

The Three Toot Heads

COLE AND RAGGY BUTT

Occasionally people get offended at my stories. I don't mean to offend anybody, but several months ago, I wrote a story about passing gas, and some people got real upset that I would discuss such a thing in public. I kinda wondered if the people who complained were some of the same people who go to a movie and laugh at sexual humor or maybe they throw out a cuss word once in a while. The way I see it, if you can't laugh about passing gas, you must be pretty bored.

Well this is one of those stories. No, it's not about passing gas, but it's about babies and poopie diapers. I have shared one of these before, but a good story is like a good steak. You can always go back for seconds.

When my daughter was a little baby and still in diapers, she was sitting on my knee in church one Sunday morning. I was supporting her bottom side with one hand and supporting her head, neck, and back area with the other, allowing her to sit upright.

My temple began to itch a little bit, so I scratched my temple with the inside heel of my palm and promptly placed my hand back under her bottom. After a few seconds, I could tell it was diaper-changing time, but the smell was extra strong. I suddenly realized not only was her diaper dirty but so was my temple! We quickly made an exit to the restroom!

My new buddy, who couldn't even say my name yet at the time, is Cole. Cole was a young man who had recently learned to walk and was trying his best to talk and was very proud he had begun potty training. I tried giving him a few spitting lessons too. All men need to learn how to spit. I don't know why men spit and women don't. It's definitely a man's thing.

One day Cole's mom walked into the bedroom and promptly found Mr. Cole standing in the middle of the bed, and he had taken his own diaper off. Quite an accomplishment for such a young man who had just begun potty training. The only problem however is it seems Mr. Cole hadn't learned the purpose of the potty yet. As he was standing in the middle of the bed in the suit he was born in, he very proudly did number one and number two on the bedsheets. Oh well, at least his heart was in it. If he can just get his brain to function and put two plus two together, he will go a long way in life, and truthfully, since that day, he has done very well.

I guess one of the worst stories I remember being told about babies and poop is about my good friend Raggy Butt. I will tell you, this story came from his sisters. I have heard one or more versions over the years, so it has to be true.

It seems when he was little and taking a bath with another family member, someone had deposited some floaties in the water. As they surfaced to the top, Raggy Butt was caught squishing them between his fingers, and he was...well, he put them in his...well... you know. Aghhh!

It kinda reminds me about the story of the little boy who took raisins to his schoolteacher every day for several weeks. One day he arrived without any raisins for his teacher, and the teacher inquired about why no raisins were left today. He promptly told the teacher his rabbit had died!

Raggy Butt

Cole

Coordinating Clothing

"Well, what are you wearing on the plane?"

"I don't know."

"Me either. I don't know if I should wear something dressy, or should I go really casual?"

"Are you taking a light jacket or a heavy one?"

"I think I am going to take one of each."

"Me too! I just can't decide."

"Are you taking a green outfit or your blue one"

"I think I may take both of them."

And on and on and on the conversation went between my wife and my mother. Finally, one of them turned to me and asked me what I was wearing on the plane. I simply answered with one word: "Clothes." They kinda got mad at me.

We were planning a family trip. My wife and I were taking my mom on a trip toward the East Coast. They were sitting at our dining room table planning details of the trip when they got on the clothes thing. I have never understood the need to coordinate clothes with other people. Can you imagine if I called one of my male friends and started asking them about what clothes they were wearing somewhere?

"Hey, Keith, I'm wearing my blue shirt and black jeans. Do you have anything that will match mine?"

"Buddy, I'm parting my hair on the right side tonight. Can you part yours, too, on the same side so we can look like we match?"

How do you think these guys would take that? They will think I flipped my fizzie if I start asking them to coordinate their clothes.

"Justin, I'm wearing my plaid walking shorts with my pink shirt. Why don't you get yours so we can match?" Jeez!

How silly does that sound, but every day across America, women are having conversations with each other about making sure their clothes match the shoes, the hair, etc. Just give me some clothes that covers the necessary parts and I'm ready to go.

My wife gets upset at me sometimes because I will wear old, wrinkled clothes when I go to town. If I am headed to the lumberyard, I could care less about my wrinkled shirt. The way I figure it, I will be so hot and sweaty by the time I get there it will be wrinkle-free anyhow! I mean what man goes to the hardware store and checks out other guys clothes? Not anybody I know. Now granted if he is extra, extra dirty, he gets bonus points because he must have had a good day of hard work, but if I see a guy walking around with pressed pants and a pressed shirt that matches the little sweat rag around his head, I kinda stay away from him 'cause he may have cooties.

It is part of the neighborhood tradition to work outside as unmatched and as unkempt as possible. Between me, my brother, and brother-in-law, we do a good job of making sure the clothing does not match. My former neighbor Larry also showed his lack of clothing proneness and few times too.

Well, a few days later, we departed the soil of Texas to other lands, and I really enjoyed the trip. Speaking of their lands, we all know that even though North Texas is on Texas soil, it takes several hours to travel from North to South. I was visited one day by two ladies from North Texas. They were in my office on business. It was my first introduction to them, and when we first began our conversations, they were a little reserved trying to figure out my personality. It didn't take them long to find out that I am a pretty laid-back, easy-to-get-along-with kind of guy. As our visit progressed, we soon began exchanging information about each other and our lives that the business matter became secondary. Their personality sold their company.

A few days after their departure, one of them wrote me back with a funny story. They had a funny experience on their flight home.

Somehow, someway, a drink got spilled in one of their purses while on the plane. Of course, there is only so much you can do, while on a flight, to clean things up. Once they landed, they made their way to the ladies' room. As the lady with the wet purse began to dig around in the bottom of the purse, she had forgotten that the day before, she had placed two large cookies in her purse for a snack. As she reached into the bottom of the purse, she felt this nasty, gooey blob of mess. She was going to throw it away, but the trash can was so full of trash, anything she deposited in the can naturally lay on top for all to see. Imagine for a moment if you walked into a restroom and saw a woman digging brown, gooey stuff out of the bottom of her purse with her hand.

Other women entering the restroom walked circles around her to stay away. Her friend abandoned her and left her to her own mess.

CUT DOORS

I have always been one to try to fix anything once. I live by the motto "If I can't fix it, at least I can break it tryin'." Well, I am being replaced. I'm feeling sorry for myself. Poor me. I'm involved in several volunteer organizations, and once people get to know me, they actually stop asking me to help them. I'm having a hard time understanding why too!

Someday I will share with you how I hooked up my gas lines in my house to the water line. A gas stove looks real cute when it starts pumping water out of the burners. It looks like a miniature fountain in a park.

Here is another story about one of my most memorable mishaps while performing my handyman functions.

I'm a hard worker. I provide for my family. I love my wife and kids. I love God, my country, and apple pie, but for some reason, people tend to love me, but they do everything they can to avoid letting me do things with my hands. It's really difficult for me to understand why.

Even the little things in life, people try to steer me away. A lot of people won't even let me make coffee. I like my coffee real strong. When we run out of a pound of coffee after only two pots, people ask me to stop making it. I keep wondering why I see people stuck to the ceiling after drinking my coffee. Anybody that I have made coffee for has never wanted a second cup.

One Christmas I received a brand-new set of carpenter tools from my mom and dad. I was proud of my tools, and I built a brand-new toolbox as my first project. I was about sixteen, and I had already begun my working career as an automechanic. I worked for Clement Patzke in Hufsmith, Texas, and I then went to work for Johnny Reeves on Kuykendahl Road. Johnny had a lady friend who needed some doors cut off at the bottom as she had bought new carpet for her home and the doors were dragging on the carpet.

I informed Johnny I would be glad to do this carpenter work as I had a new set of tools I wanted to try out.

I arrived at the lady's home and promptly removed the door and took it outside, carefully cutting off a quarter of an inch. I rehung the door and noticed it was still dragging. The door was an entry door to her bathroom and was connected to a hallway, which made close working quarters for my work.

I took the door down again and carefully marked and removed another quarter of an inch. I rehung the door, and it *still* dragged the carpet.

I removed the door again, and knowing I had plenty of room for cutting, I then removed one inch. I carried the door back into the house, and once again the door *still* dragged the floor.

The television show *Candid Camera* was real popular back then, and I really began to wonder about this door, and I slowly looked around several corners for a possible camera. I even considered the possibility of the home having a cracked foundation and was settling quite quickly.

Once again I removed the door and promptly removed two inches, knowing full well this *had* to be enough regardless of how fast this home may be settling.

Carrying the door back in, I hung it in place, and well, you guessed it, it was *still dragging!!!!*

Falling against the wall in frustration, I rested my back and head against the Sheetrock as my eyes scanned the three-plus inches of sunlight shining across the top of the door. In case you haven't caught on, I was cutting the wrong end of the door off.

The lady was real kind to me. As she tried to keep from laughing, her comment was this: "I always wanted to look out the top of my door while in the bathroom." I picked up my tools and politely dismissed myself from her home.

DIRTY SAUSAGE

"Yep, it's got grit in it all right."

"It does?"

"Yep, it sure does. I can feel it gritting in my teeth. Did it fall on clean concrete or dirty concrete?"

"Well, it's not like we washed the concrete down or anything, but there wasn't any cow manure around, that's for sure!"

"Well, you must not have washed it off too good then."

"Well, what do you expect with only one eye? I can only see half of what I'm doin'!"

"Well, Delbert, then if you can see only half of what you're doin' and I can only hear half of what I'm hearin' then I guess we might make one whole person if we work together!"

The above conversation was almost the kind of conversation my friend Delbert and I had one day when we went to the ranch together.

I hadn't been to see Leon, my therapist, in several weeks. I knew the cows had a little grass to sustain them, and I had been asking my friend Stan to go check on them every so often and put out a bale of hay. But this weekend I wanted to do some work around the house, so I made arrangements to head up there myself. I took a Friday off from work, and it was a pleasure I haven't had in a long time.

I had made arrangements for a group of people to go up with me. I was going to hire a good-sized crew and try to knock out several maintenance jobs over a three-day period. I had even planned on missing church, and now I feel guilty because none of the crew I hired showed up.

A lot of times I want to go alone to the ranch, but this weekend I decided I wanted some company. The bad thing about going to the ranch by myself is that if I ever get seriously hurt, I may have trouble getting out by myself because we are in a pretty remote spot.

Anybody who has ever been around a farm or a ranch knows an injury could result in a split second. A slip of a blade, a kickback on a saw, a crazy cow, a broken barbed wire, a swarm of bumble bees or yellow jackets, snakes, spiders, and hundreds of other things could go wrong. Sometimes a guy gets a feeling he needs somebody around. I kind of felt that way this weekend. That was why I asked Delbert to go along.

About a week prior to this particular weekend, I woke up one morning stone-deaf in one ear. My equilibrium had been a bit off. I went for testing, and fortunately my blood work and my MRI showed no signs of abnormalities. I still didn't know exactly what was wrong, but the doctor felt fairly sure it might be a viral infection that only time could heal, if ever. He had pretty much prepared me for permanent deafness in my right ear. I was feeling a bit uneasy, so Delbert went with me.

Friday and Saturday were both hot days, but Saturday afternoon, about four o'clock, I heard the faint, familiar sound of a flock of geese headed south. I knew a chill was on the way. By six, more and more of them were headed south, ahead of the supposedly cool front predicted in our area.

I like the fall and winter. I don't like the hot summertime. Fall seasons seem to bring a schedule back into our lives. School has started, the holidays are about to begin, and even though the holidays get hectic, we still have a preset schedule in our lives. We are forced inside our homes earlier each evening, and it just seems to bring a time of togetherness in most families.

By Sunday afternoon around two o'clock, the cool front had already hit Independence, Texas, and all the animals and I were feeling our oats. The cows got happy, the deer started moving, the geese were still flying, and I was able to do manual labor and not break a sweat.

The first night we arrived, I had put some link sausage on the pit for us to have for supper. I told Delbert to watch them while I went inside to shower. When he took them off the pit, they broke apart on him and fell on the concrete porch. Naturally as most men would do, he simply picked them up and washed them off, and we had a fairly good meal.

Now before any of you start fussing about the notion we would wash off a sausage and then eat it, let me point out a few facts. A sausage is wrapped in the casing, which is merely a gut. People eat apples with the skins after they have been washed, and I wonder how much dirt and dust have accumulated on them, but you still wash them off and eat them. Or how about tomatoes? Do you eat the skins? What about potato skins? These are all foods that are washed before eaten and may very well have been dropped, pooped on by flies, or rolled across the ground before you eat them. We simply wash our food and eat it. And if you're still grossed out and swear you never eat the skins because they may have had a little dirt on them, then pray tell, how can you eat eggs? What part of the body does an egg come from?

Delbert

EASTER HEIFER

During the four weeks before Easter one year, I had been taking care of a young heifer I had to bring back from the ranch. She had been injured by what appeared to be a swift kick in the shoulder by one of my donkeys. I couldn't care for her at the ranch in Independence, Texas, so I loaded her up and placed her in a makeshift pen behind my house.

On the Saturday before Easter, my family gathered together for our annual Easter celebration at my mom's house, which is next door to my place. It had always been a tradition we celebrate with a good meal and rest and relaxation. My brother and two sisters, along with the brothers-in-law, nieces, and nephews, had always been a part of this gathering. My nieces and nephews are growing up. Several of them now having their driver's license, and as I see each one of them, I can see a part of myself during my teenage years.

This year after we had our meal, a game of volleyball was played in the backyard. I watched my brother-in-law take an extended body dive for volleyball and hit the ground real hard. His oversized spare tire didn't help him any, and I knew, by the next day, he would probably really feel the hard ground in his bones. I feel safe in writing about my brother-in-law Les because he lives out of town. The only way he will read this article is if my mom sends my sister this story, and by the time I see him again, he will have forgotten I talked about his spare tire.

Another tradition we have always held is an Easter egg hunt for the young'ens. This year our young'ens are almost old'ens, and they are in this midrange state of age where the only reason they wanted to hunt Easter eggs is because there might be some money inside the egg. The candy is not an enticement anymore, but the green means something. My granddaughter is only two, and her ability to enjoy Eater egg hunting is borderline, but two of my nephews wanted to give it a try.

As always I like to make things a bit more interesting, so I was going to create a ten-dollar egg for them. The heifer I had penned up in the back area of our property was in close proximity to my mom's yard. I thought it would be fun to place an Easter egg on the back of this heifer and let the boys try to capture the egg. This young heifer is in the 350- to 450-pound range, and she was just the right size, I figured, for this makeshift rode event.

I went to my truck and pulled out the old, trusty duct tape and grabbed one of those plastic eggs. I back wrapped the tape around the egg, causing the sticky side of the duct tape to be exposed. When a person delivers cattle to the auction barn, each animal is tagged with a special number. The tags they use are actually glued onto the animal's back. They take a tube of glue and squirt some on the tag and then they actually throw the tag glue side down on the animals' back, never touching the animal. I figured I could do the same thing with this egg. I wanted to simply throw the egg on the heifer's back, expecting it to stick.

This young Brahman heifer had been in my direct care for four weeks. By nature, Brahmans are a nervous breed, skittish and sometimes wanting to fight. She had been in my direct care for the past four weeks, and she had become very docile, and she had not given me any trouble for the past couple of weeks. I climbed into the pen, and with one toss of the back-taped egg, I hit her on the back. But all kinds of chaos was started. In one single leap, she jumped five feet high onto one of the cattle panels I had her enclosed in and tore it down like a stack of matches. She immediately bolted from the yard and stood straightway on the middle of Hufsmith Road, staring at the oncoming cars.

As soon as this heifer hit the fence, my entire life flashed before me. For the past four weeks, I had thought I had broken the life-long curse I had carried with animals and me. It never fails that if I bring an animal home from the ranch, they are going to get out and attempt to run away, and with only two days left before I take her home, this young heifer was about to possibly cause some serious injury or damage to someone.

Some of the people that had moved into this area had no clue about driving near animals. I had seen too many people fly by horses and cattle on the road without giving it a second thought. As soon as the family saw what happened, the men of the family jumped into action. Les, Sonny Wayne, Code Man, Brandon, Justin, and Nathan all took off chasing this calf down the road. I think my brother Keith and brother in law Ken joined in as well. My neighbor Larry and his wife saw what had happened, and they hopped into their truck to give chase too. Cars were stopping, and some continued to fly by. People, cars, and one animal were all over the road. She ran about two hundred yards east on Hufsmith Road. I jumped on my four-wheeler and wanted to get in front of her and cut her off. I knew that if she ever got down as far as Burroughs Park, we might never see her again. We soon got her pushed into our neighbor's horse farm. When the horses saw this strange animal and she saw them, panic once again erupted. These fine show horses started bucking and kicking and running crazy, and all I could think of was the potential loss of monetary value to these horses if one of them were to have injured themselves. The heifer finally ran off the road and inside a fenced area, I went back to the house to get my truck and trailer. We had her cornered around the neighbor's barn and the guys were holding her at bay when she suddenly found a gap in the fence and off she took again. When I got back with my rig and saw the chaos again, I seriously thought about putting this heifer down due to the potential hazard she was causing.

As we chased and corralled, ran and waved, hollered and pushed with human chains, one of the ranch hands next door finally got a rope on her and the event was over. My son, Justin, tried his hand at roping her, too, but he ropes like his dad and his grandfather. Not at all. I forgot to teach him you couldn't stand on the end of your rope while throwing it.

We had no loading chute, but as I pulled from the front with the rope and Les and Justin lifted from the rear, we finally got her loaded. She was taken back to the ranch in short order. She is doing fine, but not so for Uncle Les.

After taking an extended body dive at the volleyball, he pulled his back a little while lifting the heifer into the trailer, and I think he also cut his arm. Once we arrived back at the house with the truck and trailer, he stepped off the trailer and twisted his ankle. Poor guy. I just hope he doesn't abandon me next Easter as it seems this brother-in-law always gets everybody into some kind of mess.

FALLING LIGHTS IN THE CHURCH HOUSE

My various goof ups in life have been discussed on many occasions. These mess ups have caused me concern because people tend to shy away from allowing me to help them on projects once they hear my stories.

I have hooked up my water lines on my house to my gas lines. I told you how I cut a door off at the wrong end, only to leave a big gap in the top of the door. There are many, many more stories to tell. Another story of my life occurred back in the early to mideighties.

The church I attended went through a change of ministers. This occurs throughout churches all the time, and it takes a few months for all people to settle in to the new personalities involved.

During the first week or two of Brother Carpenter's new tenure, he called a church workday, and as always, I was one of the first ones to show up, ready and willing to take on any task assigned to me.

This story is so bizarre, I'm sure some of you will question its authenticity, but I assure you I would not make up stories that involve a man of the cloth.

Brother Carpenter didn't know me from Adam at the time, and he was taking his time with the various men of the church, getting to know all of us, and we were telling stories about the church and the people in it.

One of my duties assigned was the reinstallation of a burned-out light bulb in the very top of the beamed ceiling in our sanctuary.

When changing the bulb, we used a long aluminum pole with a suction cup on the end designed for this purpose.

Now keep in mind, Brother Carpenter was still in the mode of learning the different personalities in his new congregation, and the only way to find out anything was to connect himself to the preferable grapevine that runs through all churches. Never mind he could have studied us on our own merit. No, sirree, the guys at church had to let him know right away to stay away from Clifford.

Several of the men were gathered at the front of the church talking to Brother Carpenter, and they had surrounded me, watching me maneuver this pole into position. As I was about my work of unscrewing the bulb, they began to caution Brother Carpenter about allowing me to do any work at all around the church house. They were laughing and cutting up while telling him the cut door story, the gas-water line story, and several others. They kept cautioning him about allowing me to do any work at all with my hands. He was laughing at the stories with them, and I really think he just felt I was the kind of guy who could take a joke and simply thought these guys were exaggerating a little when—God was our witness—the entire light fixture I was working on came crashing to the floor at the same time I was speaking the words "Oh, come on, guys, I'm really not that bad!!!!!"

Not only did the light fixture fall to the floor, but the two wires that were connected to the fixture in the ceiling arched together, and a small blue flame began emitting from the ends of the wires. In a moment's panic, we wanted to put the fire out but realized we had no way to reach the flame twenty foot in the air. The light-blue flame quickly burned itself out, and the panic was over.

I continued to volunteer for church work, but when I did, Brother Carpenter kindly thanks me for volunteering, excuses me from workday, and promptly relates the stories to the rest of the congregation, cautioning them in a very priestly fashion about the dangers of allowing Clifford to volunteer his time to work with his hands.

Years have passed, and I have now aged to the point that I feel I have a lifetime excused absence for hands-on church work. Can I be of service to you for small handyman projects?

High Ceiling

FIGHTING OVER MY UNDERWEAR

I need to start this story with a warning. This story should be read by men only. Women won't understand it, so they probably won't like it at all, so if you are a female reader, you need to put this paper down and walk away. (I wonder how many women would really do this, but I've warned ya.)

Years ago, we were planning an annual get-together for the men of my mom's side of the family and our side of the family at the ranch. It was a time we all enjoyed. We started our head count, and we started buying our supplies, and the occasion took me back several years ago about one of those previous weekends. The time was well spent with my uncle Marvin Dale and my cousins. It was our annual event where the men from the Osgood side of the family and the Parker side of the family met one time a year and allowed the younger boys in the family free reign on anything they wanted to do (within reason, of course).

If the boys wanted to get muddy in the pond, that was okay. If they wanted to wrestle and tussle in the house, that was okay. If they wanted to have a pillow fight or jump on the camp house bed, that was okay too. Anything went within reason.

We all enjoyed the weekend of the guys getting together and just messing around. This particular year was the first year in a long time that I didn't have a major project I needed help with. In years past, the clan had helped me work cattle, build fence, clear brush, burn the pasture, and other things that went on around a small, working ranch.

Our group had changed. Some of our young men were in the service or school, and some of them had full-time jobs that would not let them attend our event every year. The extended family had other last names. Abels, Letsingers, Moores, and Crouches all rounded out the in-laws or family that attend.

This year I did have a small project, however, that I personally worked on. I had been selling, throwing away, and giving away a lot of junk. I had collected many, many miscellaneous items in my lifetime. It was always those things that I "might need someday." I had kept old blankets, pillows, nails, broken tools, broken chairs, lumber, and all sorts of things that were really and truly junk.

We had this problem in my family. If something broke here at home, we took it to the ranch to use it up there like some miracle was going to occur and make the broken item work up at the ranch. We had a large assortment of TVs, broken chairs, vacuum cleaners, and all sorts of things that did not work here, so we took them to the ranch because we might need them. Well I had been on a rampage, and I had been throwing away junk.

As I was cleaning out a closet, I found two old pairs of my underwear. Now, most of you guys understand that underwear had to be broken in. If the elastic band was too new, it might cause you to be uncomfortable. If the cloth hasn't been washed several times, it might cause irritation, and of course underwear has got to have a hole in it somewhere before it became well qualified as being broken in.

Well, these two pairs of underwear I had found were in pretty bad shape. I am a tighty-whities guy. As a joke to me some years ago, somebody took one of the pair and burned a hole in the backside to make them look like I had created a burned-out hole in the cloth by passing gas too much. They had actually hung them on the wall for a period of time so everybody could have a laugh.

The other pair was some of my pink underwear. I turned some of my white briefs into pink underwear by washing them one time with my red shop rags. I know better now because I do not wear pink underwear!

In my act of giving things away, I started giving old pieces of scrap paper or old junkie rags and books to the little cousins in the family. I would tell them they needed to keep this item forever because someday it will be worth a lot of money as antique paper or an antique book. It was just my way of having them carry this junk home, so their parents could throw it away for me at a later date.

After coming across the two pairs of my old underwear, I gave a pair each to the youngest boys in the crowd and told them they needed to keep these and sell them someday on eBay. I gave them a long bullcorn story about how I could autograph them and then when I leave this world they can become rich by selling my underwear that was once worn by their famous cousin Clifford.

I gave them all kinds of junk. Stuff that their parents will really, really appreciate and love me forever since I shared my wealth of junk with my family.

Later that night, all the men were sitting around the kitchen table talking when suddenly the two smallest of our group got into a tussle with each other. The commotion got louder and louder, and soon they started chasing each other, and then the noise created became a noise of anger instead of fun. As the two boys ran round and round the house, suddenly the next thing we saw was Tyler dragging Dylan across the kitchen floor with something in each of their hands. As I looked closely, it was my pink pair of underwear. They were fighting over my underwear.

It's nice to be loved.

Four-Wheelers Don't Float!

I saw something one day on the internet that made me shake my head in disbelief. A guy had taken his Hummer through water so deep it actually covered the rooftop. He had to hold his breath while driving. Surprisingly the thing still ran, and I guess he got it out okay. I then suddenly realized that while this guy must have a lot of money to burn, I couldn't criticize him too much when yours truly sank his own four-wheeler several years ago. Four-wheelers do not float.

I am the type of guy who would never aggravate anybody. I would never, ever pick on or tease anyone or prod someone into a dare. I am a very straightlaced, no-nonsense kind of guy. I would never goad or dare a group of young boys into anything. Growing up, as a child, I was always the quiet type. I never spoke my mind, and I was always extremely well-behaved. I never got into trouble, and I never tried anything outside the norm. I cannot believe that some of my family members are laughing at me and are accusing me of paying the price for some of my past deeds. I would have never done anything to any of them to try to get them into trouble. I am very sad that Ryan, Nathan, Cody (a.k.a. Centerfold), Sonny Wayne, Brandon, Cooper Dale, Tyler Dale, Dillon Dale, Richard Dale, and Colton Dale are trying to tell everybody I was teasing them one past weekend. I would never do anything like that. (And if you believe me, then let's talk a land deal on a bridge to nowhere.)

I have the pleasure once in a while to spend time at our ranch with the guys. For several years, my family and the Osgood clan have been enjoying each other's company at our ranch in Independence, Texas. We now go to their place in Milano, Texas. It gives each of us a time to relax, visit, reminisce, and tell family lies to each other. Of course I would never participate in telling tall tales. It's not in my nature.

One of the highlights of our trip is the chance to ride our four-wheelers in the mud. Several years ago, I started a little game with the younger boys called Follow the Leader. The kids think you always have to drive fast, but when I am the leader, I like going at a slow pace through deep water and heavy mud.

My four-wheeler and one belonging to Brian Dale are actually four-wheel drive. The rest of them are rear-wheel drive only. Of course, our four-wheelers can take on a heavier load than theirs can.

The boys started following me and Darren Dale through the mud, and each time we made a pass through the pond, we would move over a foot or two and get just a little bit deeper. I would never tempt the younger boys to follow me. I would never call them chicken and squawk at them like my wings were flapping. They are accusing me of this, but anyone who knows me can rest assured I would never tease the boys at all.

Pass after pass, Darren Dale and I went through the mud very kindly, asking them to join us. Unfortunately for me, as you can see by the picture, I moved over just a little bit too far. Of course, the boys had a good laugh. My last words were "Oh no, I'm losing power!"

MY FRIEND FRENCHIE

This story will be difficult for me to present in proper perspective because it is one of those stories that you just had to be there to understand, but I'm going to give it a try.

This story is about a longtime family friend named Phillip Campise a.k.a. Frenchie. Sadly, Frenchie passed away many years ago, but the memory of this good man remains with me forever. Now some of the locals may know Phillip Jr., so don't go confusing Junior with his dad, but if you want to call him Frenchie Jr. after you read this story, it may bring a smile to his face. Neither one of these guys were anywhere near being a Frenchman. Quite to the contrary, they are Italian.

Phillip and his family attended a church together for many years along with my family. The church has been a center of our lives, and together we all remember good and bad times. It was a small church, and in a small church everybody gets to know each other in great detail. Sometimes too much detail, and that's the point of this story.

Phillip's personality was one of a quiet demeanor. I know his children will probably disagree with me, but I never found Phillip to be the type of person who was loud or boisterous. His personality had always been presented to me as a meek and soft-spoken type of man. He was rock solid in his work ethics, and he was the type of man you could depend on in most situations. I never heard him get openly angry, upset, or mean toward anyone, and he would quietly express himself in a direct and straightforward manner. He was not always the first to agree or oppose as he usually followed the lead of others and listened to all sides before jumping to any conclusions.

The church we attended had a foyer area that was rather small in size. Our church ran a constant one hundred or so people, and when church was about to start or dismiss, everybody assembled in the foyer for friendly conversation.

Our church, as with all churches, had their funny or odd parishioners who may attend the service. Now I know we are all sinners saved by grace, and I also know church is made for the sinner and not the saint, but there are a few people in this world who we all know are just downright funny or embarrassing to be around. You know the type. Maybe this person comes to church with real bad BO, and you know they have money for soap and water, and you wonder why they don't bathe. Or maybe they have a bad habit of belching out loud in public, or maybe they have one of those voices that carries halfway across the world when you are talking to them. It's just the type of people that, because of their personal habits or personalities, you don't become bosom buddies with them.

Well, we had one lady who attended our church who was this way. She was brash and loud, very outspoken and highly lacking the educational requirements needed for a first-grade reader. We loved her, prayed for her, tried to befriend her, but her ways and actions made the idea of a close friendship difficult. If you asked her a simple question, her answer left you wondering what your original question was. If you said to her how beautiful the weather was today, she would wind up telling you it was horrible outside because it reminded her of the day she got a bad infection of head lice or something.

This lady found herself in a motherly way and was extremely pregnant. It was a very hot summertime day, and the poor lady was miserable. Her due date was only days away, and she had gotten extremely large.

She walked into the foyer on this hot day and was wiping sweat off her forehead with her bare hand and slinging it into the crowd around her. As she was walking into the main part of the foyer, she began to rightfully bemoan the intense heat outside. Her comments were extremely loud, and her voice bellowed across the crowd.

Everyone could hear everything she had to say. Phillip happened to be standing alone in the crowd, and as she approached Phillip, she slapped him on the arm and in a very loud and demonstrative way. She then placed her cupped hands under her. Ah, she grabbed her, well, she placed her hands on her top part and said, "Oh, god, it's so hot, and I've gotten so big. What am I going to do with these two things Frenchie?"

A stunned silence fell over the church crowd as I looked at Phillip, and I thought he was going to melt into the carpet with embarrassment. His face turned red as he scanned the crowd, knowing that every ear had heard and saw what this lady had just done. If an apple is red, then Frenchie's face would have made the apple pale in comparison. I don't know if he even tried to think of an answer for her, but when the silence broke, we all began to express to Phillip his new nickname of Frenchie.

There is another story about Frenchie he created for himself. You know what a spoof is, don't you? It's my own interpretation. A spoof is simply a silly human mistake we all make in life. I ought to know. I have made a bunch of them. You go to church and realize you have on two different colored socks. How about going to work and seeing you have put your shirt on inside out, or how about the woman that goes into the restroom and comes out with a part of her dress tucked in her pantyhose. Those are spoofs. Silly things that happen to all humans at one time or another. I can still remember the time a woman I know and love very much walked out of a public restroom with a long trail of toilet paper stuck to the bottom of her shoe. She kind of looked like a scarecrow that was losing its stuffing. Many years ago, my mom had dropped my grandma off in front of the grocery store one day and then pulled away to park the car when suddenly Grandma came rushing across the parking lot, wobbling from side to side trying to catch my mom. It seemed she had changed shoes before going to the store and left one dress shoe on one foot and one house shoe on the other. Those are spoofs. Anyone who has never had something funny happen to themselves apparently has not lived very long. It happens to everyone. Kings or queens, presidents, and their wives all make funny human mistakes. Even a few preachers I know have preached many a sermon with an open fly.

It seems Frenchie got up one morning and wanted to brush his teeth and comb his hair. He made his way to the bathroom, he picked up either a tube of Preparation H to brush his teeth, or maybe he was going to comb it into his hair, I don't remember. Either way, I think one of his family members apparently saw his error and stopped him. Now can you imagine the ramifications of his actions? I wonder what would have happened to Frenchie if he would have doused his teeth with a good ol' lathering of some Preparation H. I wonder if his tongue would have shrunk up like a hemo—well, never mind. You get the picture. I really wonder what we would be calling him today. Mumble Mouth? What if he would have combed this stuff into his hair and his wife would have kissed him on the head? Would her lips shrink up? Would his scalp have shrunk and moved his head of hair to his upper lip or to the middle of his back? What if he would have grabbed a tube of Bengay to take care of other problems or possible medical problems down below? Would we be calling him Rocket Man when the fire down below started burning?

Living life is fun. I enjoy my time and place here on this earth, and I'm glad to know that in the end, we are all humans with human frailties and human failures, but together we can laugh about them.

Frenchie was the name he wore until his passing, and it still lives today among his old friends.

Frenchie

FRESH OR OLD

Okay. I already know that somebody is going to think I have too much time on my hands, but I have been in deep thought the last few weeks. Part of this is my wife's fault because she has asked me a couple of these dumb questions, but I want you to simply sit back and ponder on some things for a while. I will call these deer-stand thoughts or tractor-driving thoughts. Now if you have never sat in a deer stand or drove a tractor, I can tell you that deep, deep thoughts can be created while you are sitting in a deer stand or on a tractor. So here we go.

Why do we use the term "state of the art"? I'm not asking what it means because I know what it means. The question is why? What state is art in? Does this mean that art is stately? Is art in a particular state? What makes this term mean first class or top of the line? Why can't we just say something like "the best there is" or "top of the line"? Why is the word "state" used?

Next question. Why do we use the word "fresh" so much. Fresh vegetables, fresh barbecue, fresh fish, etc. If it's not fresh in the first place, why would you sell it? What would happen if our signs just stated "Barbecue for Sale"? Is just plain ol' barbecue any different from fresh barbecue? Would someone buy it if the sign stated "Day-Old Barbecue" or "Stale Barbecue"? If it's not fresh, then it must be old, so don't sell it. When does fresh become old? Do you remember when we used to advertise fresh air conditioner? Come on in for some fresh, cool air. Is inside air really fresh or has it already been

61

rebreathed? Can we really get fresh air from a can? If you get fresh with somebody, does that mean they really enjoy being around you or do they want to run?

What about the idea of something being "homemade"? We all place great emphasis on homemade products. Homemade cookies, homemade pies, homemade bread, and on and on. What is so special about baking something homemade? Look at it this way. You go to the store to buy the products. Flour, sugar, milk, eggs, and all the other products. You take them to your home, but yet they are store bought. Does taking the products home make them homier? What if you took the products from your home and then to your office, and if you have a stove at your office and bake them, will the product no longer be homemade, or will it now be "office-made"? Will it taste differently? Aren't the products bought in a store? So they really don't start out from home in the first place. Confused? Me too.

What about "made from scratch"? This one kinda grosses me out. Think about the term "scratch." I know the idea is the item is made from nothing into something, but all products start from nothing to become something in the first place, so aren't all products made from scratch in the first place? What is "scratch" anyway? Do you scratch before you start making the item? I have heard of hen scratch or chicken scratch. It's grain fed to chickens, but what is "scratch"? Flakes of skin you scratch off? Gross.

Have you ever heard the expression "cream of the crop"? Now I know what cream is, and I know what crops are, but what do they have to do with each other? Crops don't make cream, and cream ain't in crops. Cream always rises to the top. Do you really want the tops of the items you are discussing? Do we eat pineapple tops? How about the top parts of fresh corn? Good fresh corn may have a worm in the top. Does "cream of the crop" really mean the top part?

My wife's grandma Thrash brought up a good question many years ago. It's something she pondered until her passing. When she was a young girl, she had to pick cotton. She remembered very vividly the idea of going to the cotton field way before sunrise and sitting on her cotton sack waiting for the sun to rise so they could see well enough to start picking. She often asked, "Why in the world didn't we just sleep a little later and arrive at sunrise instead of sitting in the field doing nothing in the middle of the dark?"

Now I know everybody has their own ideas about these deep, deep questions, but all in all, it seems we place odd emphasis on strange words and sayings.

I need to go to the ranch and talk to my cows about all this. They usually seem interested in such matters.

Funny Short Stories

Misspoken words are sometimes funny. I want to relate five short stories to you that I still laugh at every time I think about them.

Many years ago, my wife and I were on a vacation trip. We were in need of some all-American fast food, so we found the local Burger King. As we approached the counter after waiting in a long line, my wife promptly placed her order. She said, "I'll have a Big Mac!" Needless to say, most of the patrons developed a smile on their face as I busted out with laugher. The cashier quickly reminded my wife she was standing inside a Burger King location.

A place I enjoy eating lunch sometimes is down at the local Blueberry Patch. I have had the pleasure of meeting most of the owners. As I began to leave the restaurant, Tony asked me how Leon, my bull, was doing. I said, "Well, he's okay but not in the best of shape." Tony promptly replied, "Are you going to make pork chops out of him?" We both laughed at his mistake.

When I was a little boy just learning to read, my mom took me to a drive-in for a summertime refreshment. It was a mom-and-pop drive-in location. As my mom placed her order and turned to me, I proudly announced I would have one of those free smiles. A sign posted on their window gave the prices of their items sold, and at the bottom of the sign, these words were posted: Smiles Free.

Have you ever heard the saying "You're gonna have a lot of trouble on your hands"? My wife was talking to a young lady on the phone one day. This woman was carrying her first child and was relating to my wife the emotional stress involved with pregnancy. Together, they laughed. This lady and her husband were having a new floor installed in their kitchen, and the floor crew had stood her up a couple of times in a row. She was rightfully upset at them and fussed at them and told them over the phone that if they didn't get out to her house right away, they were going to have one mad pregnant women on their feet.

My son was going on a short driving trip toward Huntsville, Texas. He has developed a pretty good mental picture of the north, south, east, and west directions in his mind. I wanted to be real sure he understood that Huntsville was north and IH-45 and IH-59 both ran in a somewhat north and south direction. I opened the map on the counter in our kitchen and announced to him, "Come over here, son, and look at this map because I want you to have a good mental picture of this in your mouth."

One story that I remember still makes me laugh at myself every time I think about it. I know you have heard the story of how sorry people feel for themselves for not having any shoes until they meet a man with no feet, or they complain about not having any gloves until they meet a man with no hands. Well, I was teaching an adult Sunday school class relating this story, and I got a bit carried away with my own comment: "I complained about not having a hat until I met a man with no head." Needless to say, I lost the attention of my class for the rest of the lesson with laughter.

HOMEWORK

From time to time, some of my friends will contact me and tell me that they laughed and laughed at a story I have told about them. Stories that they have forgotten but somehow, some-way, in the back on my mind, the story had stuck in my memory.

I can't tell you why I can remember some things about my childhood, but I enjoy sharing what I do recall. Sometimes these same friends tell me they don't remember things happening exactly the way I told it but that's okay. The story was still exposed and could be carried on to the next generation with a slightly different twist.

While my memory of the long past is good, I sometimes forget the present. I can walk from one room to another to get something, and I forget what I even came into the room for. I can be talking to somebody who I have known for years and suddenly go blank on their name. Don't you hate that? Someone greets you in the store, and they talk and talk to you, and you can't even hear what they are saying because your mind is racing through the millions of bits and pieces of your brain's memory, trying to remember their name. Or how about when you are in a group of people in public? Two people walk up to you where three or four other people are standing around. You know only both people who walked up to you, and you greet them, and then the proper thing to do is introduce them to the rest of the crowd, but you can only remember one of their names. I have gotten to the point in life where I can joke with the group and tell them I am having a senior moment and confess openly that I have forgotten their names.

When I do that, there is always a confession by others in the crowd that the same thing always happens to them, too, and I am quickly forgiven.

There is one part of my life, however, that I am completely blank about. It's homework. I have shared many occurrences about my grade school and high school days. I can remember the day I got into trouble for eraser fights. I can remember trying to smoke in the boys' bathrooms. I can remember the names of the first guys in class who developed armpit hair or the day that a certain girl wore her first bra to school. I can remember the last pops I got in high school and the name of the teacher who gave them to me. I can remember standing behind the curtains in high school and making animal noises while the teacher aimlessly looked around the room wondering if the Ag class was bringing in the animals down the hallway. I can remember putting a tack in George Thomas's chair. I can remember the day I made Myron Schroeder cry 'cause I teased him so much. There are lots and lots of things I can remember but for the life of me I cannot remember any homework! I'm sure I had some. I am sure at some point in my school day's I had to sit down and actually crack a book and study. I am sure I had to open a notebook and actually write something but…but…I just can't remember it!

The thought of copying someone else's work never entered my mind. The idea of cheating was and still is wrong, but I still don't know when and where I ever did any homework. I really and truly cannot remember ever going to a desk at home or the kitchen table and ever actually studying from grade school through high school. I am sure my Mom helped us with homework somewhere along the way but this part of my life is lost.

I never did like school too much unless I was having fun. College for me was out of the question. I would calculate the fact that while my friends left high school and went four more years to college I could be working and making money and could be ahead of the game before they ever got out of college. I will never know if my idea worked because I have since learned that money is the least of life's issues. Living and loving life itself is the name of the game and then we can learn to be satisfied with what God has given us.

One of these days, I just hope I can remember doing some homework!

I Am a Professional Baseball Player

Little League Baseball has been alive and well for many, many years. I ought to know 'cause I played baseball during the late fifties and early sixties on what is now the new Senior Field here in the city I grew up next to named Tomball, Texas.

Did you know that Tomball used to even have an adult baseball team? Yep, sure did. During the forties and fifties, a large group of men from Hufsmith and Tomball used to get together for baseball, and from what I'm told, it was a really hot league. They say most of the games were held in the open field at the old Hufsmith/Tomball/Concordia School even before the school was built. One man told me, if you knew where to look, you could probably find a treasure of old coins, jewelry, and baseballs in the field since this was one of the hot spots of the baseball world. My experience at the game of baseball was short-lived and very different, but I became a professional with a very short career.

The two coaches I had were Coach Burklin and Coach Watson, and both of these gentlemen gave me fond memories of the game with one exception. I was scared to death of the ball. I just couldn't bring myself to understand why anybody would want to stand at a plate and have someone throw the ball toward me as hard as they could, thinking full well if they threw the ball at me, I probably couldn't jump back in time. I was the kind of player who was stepping out of the box before the ball ever left the pitcher's hand.

My lack of expertise extended to the outfield as well. When a ball was hit long and high, my eyes would bounce up and down in my head as I ran toward the ball, and I would lose sight of the ball. I would get what I call "ball fever." My heart would race, my palms would get sweaty, my mouth would get dry, and I was scared to death to go after a catchable fly ball until, until one time.

I was in my usual courtesy position in right field, and a long, high fly ball was hit in my direction. In fear, I covered my eyes with one arm and extended my gloved left hand high into the air, and I began to run. I don't know where I was running, but I remember running and running hard too. With my eyes still covered, my feet in motion, and my glove high in the air, the ball fell right into my glove!

I still remember hearing the roar of the crowd as I ran into the dugout with the ball in my hand as this made the third out.

As I entered the dugout, I could still hear Coach Bill Burklin yelling to me, "Way to go, Parker!" As I moved toward the bench, Coach Watson patted me on the back and said, "Son, I don't know how you did that, but that was the best catch I have ever seen." And he handed me a quarter. I guess you could say I'm a professional player since I've been paid.

I only hope, as each baseball season begins around the world, that each coach, manager, spectator, and everyone else remembers the important point of the memories you are making for kids today will last a lifetime. Make those memories good ones.

I Want Some Food!

"Happy birthday to you. Happy birthday to you. Happy birthday, dear Clifford. Happy birthday to you." And with that, my wife broke off a piece of a day-old blueberry muffin and gave me a bite to go along with my roadside coffee.

I was celebrating a birthday many years ago, a birthday while away from Texas soil. It was my first time to ever leave the Country of Texas on my birthday, but my wife, my mother, and I enjoyed a three-day trip through parts of Pennsylvania.

It was the first time the three of us had ever traveled together out of state without other family members. We had a very pleasant time in places like Hershey and Valley Forge.

One of the pleasures enjoyed was the food. Now I am about to enter very delicate territory because the basis of this story involves my mom. It is very, very difficult to write about her because of the sensitive issues. What will her friends think? What will people think about me divulging secrets on my own mother? How will she be perceived in public? Those are all issues when writing about your own mother, but I have decided to delve into the story headfirst.

My family has always enjoyed each other's company over a good meal. Everything we do together is celebrated with good food, and a lot of the family food has always been made by my mom. As the years have progressed, many of the other ladies in our family are now supplying the same traditional dishes my mom made, each with their own style and flair.

Now I set this food thing up because with all due respect, but not only could my mom cook it, but she also enjoyed her cooking too.

During our trip, we stopped at a country buffet. Here is a listing. Pot roast, beef strips, chicken strips, chicken and dumplings, chicken potpie, fried chicken, baked chicken, dressing, buttered noodles, boiled eggs, beets, broccoli, corn, green beans, salad, tea, coffee, apple pie, apple cobbler, ice cream, and Shoo Fly Pie were on the list. Now I don't mean the buffet list. I mean on her list of things she ate. (I must admit, I might have taken some liberties to this list to emphasize my point.) I, too, had my own listing.

The food we consumed, of course, made us miserable, but after the fiasco we had at breakfast, it nearly became our only meal of the day.

I made a wrong turn on the expressway, and when you get on a Pennsylvania turnpike, there ain't no getting off for nearly twenty miles. We traveled the same road twice! That was why my breakfast and birthday cake consisted of what they call a plaza stop. It was simply a small refreshment stand and gas station on the side of the road.

The meal issue set me up for the rest of my story however. When traveling with someone who occasionally walks with a cane, a new respect is usually shown by most of the public. As a society, we tend to watch out for those who have an advanced age. So was the case while traveling with my mom.

People had a tendency to slow down a little and give us a little more space as we made our way in public places.

The following day, after eating our buffet, we had decided we wanted a Philly cheesesteak sandwich. Once again we missed our breakfast call because we had traveled in circles and missed the eating places we wanted, so it was well into the afternoon before we hit the local eating establishments for a meal. We had simply snacked on junk food to tide us over. Junk food is good, but after a while, eating junk is just what it means. Junk! You finally get tired of junk and want some real food. So it was with my mom.

We were walking down the main corridor of the local market when my wife and my mom began discussing the next meal. Back and forth, they chatted while walking, and the public was well within earshot of everything they said. It was then suggested that once again we grab a snack and save our big meal for later in the day when my mom blurted out very loudly and forcefully, "No, I want some food, and I want it now!" A hush seemed to hit the people around us as my wife and I began to receive those evil stares from people. We could feel the daggers being thrown at us in their minds because we had deprived this sweet lady some food. Never mind we had been packing away all sorts of miserable calories the whole trip. Never mind she had eaten twenty-nine-plus items from a buffet less than twenty-four hours earlier. This sweet lady walking in a public place with cane in hand was being starved.

Fortunately the conversation was laughed about between ourselves, and we felt the public's perception of us subside. We finally found an eating place. We enjoyed.

Mom

If It Were a Snake

I'm sure everyone has heard the old saying "If it would have been a snake, it would have bit me." We have all had an experience at one time or another when the obvious is slapping us in the face and we are still trying to find it hidden away somewhere. The next three short stories show you what I mean.

My little brother, Keith, was always getting the usual boyhood bumps and bruises, and his tolerance for pain was somewhat high. I think his stubbornness and bullheadedness contributed to his tolerance. I have seen him get a spanking and refuse to cry, which simply made Mom madder and madder, so she would spank him harder. I was smart enough to know if I would start crying before she even started the spanking, she would stop a lot sooner. Keith's reluctance to cry and accept pain simply meant when he did cry, he was really, really hurting, and it usually required special attention.

One day he came running into the house screaming and crying while pointing to his mouth. Mom was in a panic trying to assist him as he continued to point toward his mouth, mumbling words about a wasp. Mom forced his mouth open trying to inspect his throat area as he continued to cry and point. Mom was still in a panic as she continued searching his mouth, teeth, and throat, and I even believe she went so far as to get the flashlight to inspect deep inside his throat. He was still crying and slobbering when he was finally able to get the words out about his lip being bitten, and sure enough, once Mom quit looking on the inside of his mouth, there on his lip was a giant blister beginning to develop where the wasp had bitten him. All the time she was looking in the wrong area and had overlooked the obvious outside and not the inside of his mouth.

Another time he came screaming about his nose burning. Apparently he was messing around with a gas can, and he came running into the house pointing at his nose, crying his eyes out about his nose burning. She ran and got a wet rag and tried desperately to clean the inside of his nose out. "Blow, blow," she would tell him, and poor, little Keith would blow his nose real hard between the tears. Soon Mom ran to get a glass of water and made him snort clean, clear water into his nose to get the gas out of it. After a few more tears and a little prompting from Mom about what had happened, it was soon discovered the gas splashed on the outside of his nose and not on the inside.

One day while I was sitting at the back of the church house on a Sunday morning, I heard a loud commotion in the foyer. I heard a child choking and coughing, and I heard a female voice desperately in panic for this child. I heard her call on the name of Jesus, and I could tell this child was in serious trouble, so I bolted out the back door into the foyer to offer assistance. There was little Clifford Ford (no, no kin to this Clifford) being slapped on the back by Sister Duke, trying to dislodge a piece of candy supposedly caught in Clifford's throat.

By the time I made it through the door, Clifford was trying to get a drink of water, and she was still slapping his back. Finally after a few milliseconds, he began to holler at her because she was hurting him. It seems the piece of candy had dislodged itself several seconds earlier and she was not aware of this fact so she was still in a panic mode slapping his back while in his mind all was now okay.

It's funny now to look back at these incidents and realize they could have been tragedies, but in reality the seriousness of the event was like the old snake saying. The problems were not as great as they had seemed, and if it had been a snake, somebody would have gotten bit.

ISBELL'S

I have always tried to tell my children that everything we do in life can have an impact on others. Somewhere, somehow, the chain that connects all families can be hurt or be helped by the actions of one person within that family. That chain extends to all people, and the actions of one person toward another can actually change the course of lives among people. It seems that regardless of all the good you may do in life, if you mess up one time, people will only remember you for the bad thing you did and forget the good.

I know that's kinda deep, but the actions of one couple in town has changed the course of my life to the good. In this case, there is only good that I can relate to this family.

I have told stories of my memories of Main Street, Tomball, Texas, on many occasions. My memories are from the midsixties to the seventies, and several buildings in town have special meaning to me. One of those locations is 710 Main Street.

During my high school days, this location was a hamburger fast food location. It was owned by a wonderful couple named Margie and Ernest Isbell. Mr. and Mrs. Isbell were middle-aged when they started the location, and they had experienced a lot more of life than I had as I was simply a high school kid with no experience in the real adult world. The world of bills and taxes, business and home maintenance, and all those things weren't even part of my thought process at that time.

Mrs. Isbell hired a young lady to work at their location. As time passed and through other activities, this same young lady caught my attention, and soon my heart was wrapped up in this girl.

We both attended Tomball High, and like most kids during those days, we had to earn our own spending money. I was about ten months older than her and two classes ahead of this gal, so I was an "older man." I had the financial responsibility of my owning my truck, and since I was a guy, I was also responsible to pay for all dates. I also enjoyed playing pool up at Mrs. Alice's Place, too, so making money was very important to me.

I have been pretty much self-employed most of my life with just a few jobs ever working for others. I spent a year or so working for Herb Kleimann at the meat market on Tuwa, and I also spent time raising tomatoes to sell to Mrs. Goodson. I tried worm farming, and I also sold sassafras tea one summer. I cleaned dozers at TT Construction, and I even tried selling barbecue, blackberries, cane poles, and scrap metal. I welded barbecue pits, and I built trailers. I raised rabbits, hogs, and cattle. I did mechanic work for Clement Patzke and Johnny Reeves, worked at Lamberts Grocery, and mowed freeways for Johnny Bonds. I hauled hay behind guys like Homer Hildebrandt, alongside Mike Reist. I did all this, all hoping to make a buck. I have worn many hats in my young career. I even sold fencing for a company and tried my hand at carpentry work prior to and during my high school days.

My self-employment allowed time at odd hours of the day to go to Isbell's for refreshment, but the truth was I simply wanted to spend time near the new love of my life. Looking back, I can see now that my being at their place of business where this girl worked probably hindered the workflow in some manner, but not once do I ever remember Mr. or Mrs. Isbell asking me to leave. I soon developed a taste for the nickel cup of coffee only because it was the cheapest thing on the menu, and I would spend a lot of time drinking coffee or simply loitering at the counter to talk sweet nothings with this girl. My heart was lovestruck, and by all rights, Mrs. Isbell could have asked me to leave, but she didn't. I am sure that deep down in her heart, she knew she was seeing a new love develop before her eyes. I would even guess that sometimes she would go home and have a private chuckle with Mr. Isbell and discuss the issue of Clifford and the hired help, but not once did she discourage me or run me off. She allowed her employee and me to spend time swooning over each other on her clock.

That has been over forty-five years ago, and I am proud to say that I can now wake up each and every morning looking into those same blue eyes of this girl who I used to spend time with at Isbell's.

Thank you, Mrs. Isbell. Thank you for your patience and understanding as you saw this young love develop. Your actions have created new families and touched the lives of many.

Mr. and Mrs. Isbell

JOY TO THE WORLD!

J oy to the world! Peace on earth! Goodwill toward men! Joy, peace, and goodwill. These are three words that were penned in the Bible before shopping malls and megasuperstores.

I went to our local Walmart during the Christmas rush one year and saw an event that made me chuckle about those three words.

During the past several years, I'm sure we can all attest to the fact that a lot of common courtesies have went by the wayside. It's sad but true. There was a time when real men removed their hats or caps before entering a building. There was a time when a man would open a door for a woman and in return women would politely say, "Thank you." Men would give up seat for a lady, and most everybody would give up their seat for a pregnant woman. We would all say ma'am and sir to each other, and the young people would always address their elders by Mr. or Mrs. until instructed to do otherwise. "Thank you" and "you're welcome" were part of our everyday vocabulary. Some people call it Southern hospitality, and I personally still adhere to the old rules of etiquette. It's sad, however, that in today's society these things are missing because each time we lower our standards a little here, another courtesy also tends to fall away, and our standards get lower and lower and lower.

Look at our driving habits. Have they improved? Our parking habits, our walking habits, our talking habits, and many other things have moved further and further toward the lowered bar of living, and I think a lot of it has to do with the "me first" attitude.

I was walking on the parking lot of Walmart a few days ago when I heard a man hollering something from his truck. His window was down and his arm was hanging out the window, and he was thrashing and waving his hands muttering something about the women parked in front of him. He was driving down the parking lot aisles, and a woman in front of him was waiting on a parking spot. Number one, she didn't have her blinker on to indicate to him her intentions. Now I know some of you think I'm being silly, but if people would just use the signal indicators to indicate what you want to do with your car and this guy might have had a little more patience. Remember, they are technically called indicators and not blinkers. They indicate your intentions of what you want to do with your car! After hearing his mutterings, I stopped to watch. For about thirty seconds, he was hollering out the window, "All I want to do is get out of this parking lot, and she has it all tied up!" Common courtesy and common sense would tell me that if I were waiting for a parking spot, I would be pulled over to the right-hand side of the traffic lane so people could pass me on the left, but not this woman. Her car was stopped right in the middle of the centerline, and she was waiting on the people in a parked car so she could take their spot. That was fine, but she lacked the courtesy to think about the people behind her. Thirty seconds turned to one minute, and the traffic behind her had increased to six stopped cars. Six cars went to eight, and then within another thirty seconds, the people trying to get off the main road were blocked. It was becoming a dangerous situation, and all the while the man in the truck was still yelling and hollering because he couldn't pull around her to get off the lot. Another woman walking toward her car saw the situation, and she politely walked up to the lady's car that was blocking the traffic and gently tapped on her window as the lady was looking at herself in her vanity mirror waiting for her parking spot. The lady explained to her she was making the traffic situation really bad, and the woman in the car simply shrugged her shoulders as if she didn't care and rolled up her window and continued to wait, and not one time did she make any attempt to move over just two feet so everybody could pass her.

After watching this thing play out for about two minutes, I was almost to the point of going over to this lady's car myself and asking her to move. She had no clue about the problems that she was causing, and by now it seemed obvious to me she was part of the "me first" generation. She really didn't care. She finally got her parking space, and the congestion was finally cleared without further incidence.

I turned and walked away and began to hum the tune of "Joy to the World." I chuckled out loud wondering how many people today are really joyful about Christmas and happy about New Year.

Make one of your next year's resolutions to be a little more courteous this year. Watch out because it can become contagious.

KEITH AND MY JACKET

The various holidays bring out the best and worst of families. Most people become more lovable during the holidays, but some families heighten their bitter feuds during these times and never come together for the real joy of Christmas.

I'm very blessed with a family that doesn't argue or fight. I lived next door to my parents and my brother, and one sister lived two doors down for a large part of my life. I had another sister who lived a short distance away, and I see my family members often enough to let them know I care but less enough to stay out of each other's business. I can truly say I don't ever remember, as adults, a family feud.

Now when I say we have never fought, I mean this from a blood battle, in-your-face type of argument that destroys lives and reputations, but we have in fact had our days, as kids, arguing over toys, wrestling just to be wrestling, and getting into the petty kid arguments as all siblings have.

There are a lot of stories I can tell, but the one Christmas story I remember most was about my mean, little brother, Keith.

Keith was a bullheaded little sneak when he was younger. (Hadn't changed much either.) He took after my dad. Stubborn, sneaky, and never said "I'm sorry" but kind and loving in a quiet way. Always available to help but wouldn't offer until asked, but when I say stubborn, I mean so stubborn he could break his teeth while pulling tenpenny nails and swear it didn't hurt.

One Christmas about sixty or so years ago, I got a brand-new motorcycle jacket. Solid black, imitation polyester vinyl, with shiny, silver zippers from the collar down to each cuff and a couple in between. That jacket made me top stud. I was the hot dog of Hufsmith, Texas, and that jacket put an armor round me that made me feel like I could whip anybody. My little rib-caged, scrawny body with Dumbo flopping ears was turned into the coolest dude who made the future Easy Rider look like Donald Duck. I was top dog. I didn't own a motorcycle at the time, and I have no idea what made me want this jacket, but when I received this gift I was very happy, and it was all mine.

I guess Keith was jealous. Keith was the kind of kid who made up his mind to do something, and he'd do it. His stubbornness made me think back to one time he came in crying one day and said his turtle died. When we asked him what happened, he blubbered and slobbered, and in between the heavy upheaval sobs, he said he didn't want it any more so he smashed it. Talk about a made-up mind, wow! But nonetheless, for some unknown reason, he felt that I shouldn't have that motorcycle jacket.

I really don't think my teasing and taunting had anything to do with it. I really don't think my rubbing it in his face a few times caused any harm, and the memory is still as clear as day.

It was a cold day shortly after Christmas, and our old butane heaters were warming the house. Suddenly a strong smell of burning rubber began to permeate the air. Rushing to my mom and dad's bedroom, the family found my new motorcycle jacket in a small pile of melted blobs dripping from the sides of the heater.

Boy was Keith in trouble. I can still see Mom smoking the backside of his Fruit of the Looms, and the streak marks she left sure wasn't what we now call "tracks" in your underwear. She spanked him and he cried and spanked him and he cried some more as she kept insisting Keith apologize for his actions. The stubborn little bugger kept shaking his head no and never to this day has said, "I'm sorry." He was bullheaded.

Mom cried 'cause she had to correct him, and she cried 'cause the money was lost. It was one of those spankings that said this hurts me more than it hurts you, but Keith never did say, "I'm sorry."

That's a Christmas I'll never forget. I still love you, Bubba. Mom's gone now and I am sure she is in Heaven. So get the belt, Mom. Keith hasn't changed!

Left to Right. My Sister Gail, My Dad, Keith, My sister Glenda, My Mom and That's me on the right! I'm still upset about my jacket! Keith is being held in place by my Dad.

LITTLE BOY WAVING HIS
HAND UNDER THE DRESS

D ads will laugh at this story. Moms will say, "My sweet little
son would never do that!" Sorry, ladies, yes, he would too!
Boys grow into men, and from about the age of five,
little boys develop a real strong interest in their female counterparts,
and that interest never leaves. Even men well in their eighties have
told me the heart is willing but the body is weak. My philosophy of
little boys works like this. At about the age of five or six, the male
brain begins to drop in the body. It moves from the head to the eyes,
from the eyes to the mouth, and onward down the body until it set-
tles in the middle at certain body parts. It remains there until maybe
the sixties, seventies, or even later in a man's life, and then it start to
move upward again.

If a study were done on little boys in grade school, I'm sure you
will find that boys drop their pencil on the floor many, many more
times than girls do. It's not that they are more fumble fingered; they
just find more things to see while peering from the floor up.

Being a man myself, I like to watch little boys because I can tell
you what they are going to do even before they realize themselves
what they are about to do. The turned heads, the quick stare, the fast
glance, the posturing of yourself in the right position to see what you
are not supposed to see on a girl are all things little boys do while
growing up, wondering and wondering if there really is a difference.
I'd bet if some of you ladies were to ask the man in your life if he

could remember the name of the girl in his grade school class who wore the first bra, they could probably remember.

Several years ago I was doing some heavy-duty shopping with my wife in a large department store. The reasons I call it heavy-duty shopping is because my job is to lean against all the clothes racks and hold them up while my wife shops. I enjoy standing in a department store watching people.

I was standing in the dress shop, and the store had a mannequin displayed on a pedestal wearing a dress. I don't know if anyone but we men have noticed, but mannequins have become more physically correct over the past several years. This particular female mannequin was dressed in a long, silky dress, and the base it stood on was about two feet off the floor. In other words the feet would hit you about thigh high.

A little boy about six or seven years old came around the corner by himself, and he sheepishly looked around to see if his mom was watching. She had her back to him.

The little boy approached the mannequin and got real close to the base, standing very straight and erect, almost as if he was at attention. He quickly glanced over his shoulder back at his mom, and knowing she was not looking, he bent over and took a peek under the mannequin's dress. He quickly stood upright and erect again and looked again to see if Mom was watching. She wasn't, and again he very quickly glanced up the mannequin's dress, taking just a split second longer than the first time. By this time, I was already hiding behind the rack of dresses laughing my head off at this curious little fellow. Again very upright and erect, he glanced at his mom, and this time, instead of bending over, he simply ran his hand way up the mannequin's dress and took off running as if he had accomplished his mission. It was a very quick wave of the hand under her dress, and off he went. I couldn't contain myself, and I'm sure if someone would have seen me, they would have thought I was crying, but I was laughing so hard tears came to my eyes.

This little boy had taken a large step in his life by moving closer and closer to becoming someone's husband, father, or grandfather. His natural curiosity had gotten the best of him, and he had accomplished his mission of wondering what was under that mannequin's dress.

I'm sure as he gets older, and if he remembers this, he will laugh at himself for a boyish act. He will probably be as disappointed as I was the first time I got to go into the girls' bathroom as an eighth grader to empty the trash cans. As I entered the room that had been off-limits as a seventh grader, I was disappointed to see it looked just like the boys' bathroom. I don't know what I expected, but another step in my life had been made, and here I sit today telling everyone about it.

MISSPOKEN WORDS

S ome days I put my mouth into gear before engaging my brain. This happened to me twice one time, and both moments were quite humorous. Both of these events happened in local establishments, but I dare not mention their names. I'm trying to protect the innocent.

On Halloween day, one local lending institution had all their employees follow a Hawaiian theme for their costumes. Coincidentally, I had made a decision to dress up as a vacationer. Now I can hear many of you wondering how can Clifford dress as a vacationer, but I know all of you have seen these guys at one time or another. I donned a round-brimmed straw hat and put on the ugliest, colored shirt I had. I put on a pair of multicolored shorts and placed a camera around my neck. I then added an accessory of flip-up sunglasses, a fanny pack, and long black knee socks, and my best wing-tipped dress shoes. I know all of you have seen at least one of these guys while traveling.

After learning of the bank's dress theme for Halloween, I decided I would visit the ladies at the bank and have a good laugh or two. When I went into the bank, I was greeted with laughter, and one of the ladies took a picture with me standing side by side against a fake backdrop of a beach. As an added accessory to my outfit, the ladies gave to me a Hawaiian lei, and it really capped off my costume. I then left the bank thanking them for the lei and went and had lunch with one of my pastors and a group of men from the church. When my pastor saw me, he didn't react too much, thinking it was not too unusual to see me dressed this way. He understands I sometimes have a screw loose, and I guess he thought this was my normal work clothes.

As I made my way back to my office and continued with my workday, I had a telephone conversation with one of my friends named Bob. Bob had asked me how my day had been thus far, and I told him of my shenanigans at the bank, and we both laughed. Toward the end of my conversation, I then expressed to him, and I quote, "Yeah, and the girls at the bank gave me a free lei." There was a moment of silence on the phone when Bob calmly said, "Wow, Clifford, that's interesting." After realizing what I had said and how I had said it, we both began a great deal of laughter.

A few days later, I was visiting a local travel agency, buying tickets for my wife and me to celebrate one of our anniversaries, and we were headed out of town. It was number 29, if I recall correctly.

The ladies at the travel agency know me and know my memory is sometimes very, very short, and they began to emphasize to me that I really need to keep track of my tickets. "Don't lose them, Clifford." Then one of the ladies jokingly asked me, "Do we need to pin a note to your underwear so you won't forget?"

To which I quickly quipped back, "I'm not wearing any underwear." I was trying to be funny and witty.

A split second of stunned silence fell over me for saying such a thing. It just fell out of mouth, but I was trying to be funny. It wasn't true or anything, but I thought it would be a great shocker. As I looked around, there were seven or eight people in the room staring straight at me, and we all began laughing real hard. I quickly left, only to return to try to straighten the story out by letting them know that I did in fact have on underwear, but I was trying to be funny. It was one of those times that the more I explained, the deeper it got. I'll never reveal if it's boxers or briefs.

MR. WASHINGTON'S
SINGING HEIFER

T hings happen in this life that can be observed by persons and carry completely opposite meanings. One person thinks an issue may mean this, and another person may think it means something totally opposite. Then you will have those who see something in between.

During my lifetime, I have had many occurrences that have made me question why God has placed me in certain situations. I have written about some of them in the past. What I'm trying to say is that sometimes events that occur make me wonder if God is trying to send us a message. This may be one of those stories. I hope you see the same things I see in this particular story.

I had a good friend in Butlers Crossing named Clemmie Washington. Mr. Washington and I had known each other for many years, and I had purchased a few head of cattle from him from time to time. I even wrote a story one time about him and his sister. Sadly, I lost my friend a few years ago when he passed away.

Mr. Washington always had animals around his property. Cows, chickens, dogs, horses, and other animals made his property home off and on for many years. He was a good-hearted man who provided care to animals. He also knew that God gave man dominion over animals, and he used animals for the betterment of himself and his fellow men.

A local church had contacted Mr. Washington to ask him if he could provide an animal during the Christmas holiday for their live manger scene. He owned a young Brahman heifer that was halterbroken, and he said he would be happy to help.

By nature the Brahman breed is a very high-strung, nervous type of animal. They are generally excellent breeding animals because they are a very hardy lot and they protect their young very well. A lot of them are jumpers, and therefore I personally have only owned one or two of these animals in my life. I personally don't like a high-strung, nervous animal on my property, but this heifer that Mr. Washington owned had never given him a moment's trouble. Well, she did knock him down one time by accident. It seems he got between her and the feed bucket in close quarters and she thought she had the right of way, but otherwise she had been an excellent animal.

Mr. Washington delivered his pet to the church property, and they tied her next door to the live manger scene. The entire property was set up somewhat like a small village during the time of Christ, and Mary and Joseph along with the baby Jesus were all posted in their positions under the straw hutch. People touring the village were carried from point to point by a wagon, and at each location, the wagon would stop and people would sing Christmas songs.

As the village became alive with a lot of activity, a young lady from the church caught up with Mr. Washington and told him he needed to come look at his calf. I'm sure in his mind he thought the animal might have been nervous or something and could possibly be acting up, however, when he arrived at the location, the heifer was standing at attention, staring straight at the baby Jesus in the manger. The animal's eyes were actually fixated on the Jesus character and seemed to be paying silent homage to the overall scene. As people would arrive at the site, they would start singing Christmas carols, and this heifer would start bellowing in singsong fashion as if it were trained on cue. The people would sing, and it would sing too. When they stopped, it would stop. It was almost as if God himself had placed his hand on this animal and was commanding its very being.

When Mr. Washington saw this animal acting in such a strange way, he began to reflect on a scripture found in the bible from Luke

19. It refers to our responsibility to offer to the world the word of God. It provides us a warning that if we do not praise God and spread his word, he could command the very rocks to cry out with praise and worship. If you think about this, that's real heavy thinking. How would you like to be replaced by a rock? Was God sending us a message? Was he reminding us again of his power to overcome all evil? Was he reminding us once again of the love of Him and Him alone, and he should be the number one thought in our lives? Have we allowed this world to overcome us with worldly things so much that he used a cow to bring a message home?

As for me and my house, we are going to take the hint loud and clear. I may not have a great singing voice or be able to give great speeches, but I'm sure not going to let a cow take my place.

MY HAIRDRESSER

I woke up this morning feeling extra tired. I tossed and turned all night long. My knees hurt, my back hurts, and my head is feeling all scratched up.

Last night I went to my weekly hair appointment at the local beauty shop. Yes, men, I have to admit, I have my hair done each week and usually on Tuesday nights. I have been doing this for about the last two or three months, and I figure I will continue until my hairdresser develops a streak of modesty.

The shop is a one-woman shop and very private. Only two other people know about the shop, being my wife and daughter. The prices have been up and down over the last few weeks. When I started visiting the shop, the lady charged me sixty and ninety. The next week, she wanted to charge me sixty, forty, and ninety. A couple of times she has actually tried to give me money when I had no change due me, but last night when I asked her how much it cost to get my hair done, she only said six dollars. I gladly paid the six dollars and settled in for a nice, relaxing hairdo. Wow! Talk about inflation.

The shop is located in my own home, so all I have to wear is an old T-shirt and a pair of cutoffs. The place is extremely casual.

Actually my hairdresser normally stays in her birthday suit. Her moments of modesty vary. One moment she runs screaming through my house from one room to the next in her birthday suit and then next she has to have a big towel around her. When she does my hair, she will not allow me into the salon unless she is submerged in a tub of water.

My hairdresser's mode of operation is very unusual. The facilities we use are actually a bathtub and not a chair. In order to get my hair done, I have to place one towel or pad on the hard floor for my knees and another towel on the edge of the bathtub to rest my arms and chin on. I hold my head over the edge of the tub while my hairdresser does her wonderful work.

Normally my hair is wetted down with a squeaky fish. She chuckles as she holds the toy in the water and presses all the air out of it. She claims the fish "pooted." Then she releases her grip on the fish and allows the squeaky toy fish take in water that she then squirts on my head. Never mind the water may be a week old and stale and stagnant. She's happy, so I'm happy.

My hair is patted down with a wet washrag, and the soaping process begins. First it's a bar of soap, then a squirt of liquid soap. More bar soap and more liquid soap. Oh, look, there's some cold cream. Let's apply some of that. Oh, there's another kind of liquid soap. Let's put some of that on too. More bar soap, more liquid soap, a mixture of bubble bath soap, and soon she has me lathered from the top of my head to the middle of my back. All the while I'm resting my head on the tub and enjoying the talented hands at work. I'm very much like an old dog. You scratch my head, and I will stay still for a long time. She's happy, so I'm happy.

After the soaping process comes the combing process. Her method becomes somewhat rough during this time. I have on occasion thought I felt the teeth of the comb breaking off in my scalp. More than once I have thought I felt a warming sensation of blood running from my head, but so far this hasn't happened. An occasional knock or lump on my head from a waylaid brush has also occurred. I still sit very still, allowing her to create this hairdo for me. I will never complain. She's happy, so I'm happy.

Once the combing is complete, then the styling begins. Parting my hair in various ways, she combs and combs, scrubs and scrubs, combs and rubs my hair until she finally announces, "I'm done!"

By now my knees are hurting and my shoulder blades are burning from being bent over the tub for so long, but that okay with me. The water that started out being warm on my hair is now almost ice cold.

As I stand up to leave, my wife, who has been nearby has to grab a camera to take a picture of my new style. Never mind I have a mass of soap running down my face and my back is soaking wet, I am still happy. Never mind I can't let her see me wash the stuff from my hair. Never mind we used a half bottle of shampoo and most of the bubble bath. She's happy, so I'm happy.

As I exit the room, my wife takes over so my hairdresser can get out of the bathtub. She is of the opinion that if she is hidden in the water, it's okay for a man to enter the room. So as I leave the room, she goes running to the open arms of my wife who is holding a large towel. She catches her and play tosses her on the bed. She snuggles her up and dries her off as I make my way to the living room. I have to carry a bath towel with me because my hair is still dripping wet.

I settle back into my easy chair with the towel wrapped around my head when my hairstylist enters the room in her nightgown. She smiles at me, and she runs and jumps in my lap. She snuggles into my chest, and I can smell the fresh aroma of baby powder. We spend a few moments together in each other's arms in silence. Finally, she breaks the moment with a request that I get on the floor and play puppy.

My knees are already aching, and my back is still burning, and the soap has turned my eyes bloodred, but that's okay with me. This dog enjoys playing like I'm young again.

My Wishes

Okay, okay, now listen up. The wishes you are about to read are my own wishes. These wishes have nothing to do with my wife or family's thoughts and nothing to do with anything from anybody other than myself. You can call me wrong, prude, silly, or just downright dumb, but these are my own personal comments. Some people make New Year's resolutions. These are not my resolutions. They are simply wishes. In random order and with no rhyme or reason, these are my wishes.

I wish texting in public would become illegal and unpopular unless someone would make a screen that did not light up every time the phone was opened. It really gets under my skin to be in a low light or darkened location like a movie or a quiet restaurant, when all of a sudden your eyes are blasted with light by the person in front of you who is texting. If I knew I wouldn't get thrown in jail, I would like to stare over that person's shoulder and read their messages out loud.

I wish talking on the cell phone and texting would be banned while driving or within a hundred feet of other human beings.

I wish somebody would invent a legal device that shuts down the motor of a tailgater who gets within two car lengths of the back of your vehicle.

I wish parking lots did not have stripping. You would be allowed to park any place and in any position you wanted. By having the stripes removed, I could not get upset at people who double park.

I wish underwear, both male and female, would no longer be used as outerwear, and I also wish it were not illegal but encouraged to give someone a wedgie if you saw the tops of their underwear coming out the top of their pants.

I wish they would quit making cars that go a hundred miles an hour when the speed limit has never been that high in my lifetime.

I wish people would stop using camouflage clothing as fashion wear. My toes are getting real sore when I stub them on people's camouflaged shoes, and my knees are aching because I keep falling down when I trip over people who are in camouflaged clothes. I just can't see them.

I wish the words "Yes, ma'am," "No, ma'am," "Yes, sir," and "No, sir" were part of a mandatory school curriculum. If a child fails to learn these words and properly use them at appropriate times, then we should be allowed to keep them in the same grade until they learn otherwise.

I wish all men would learn to remove their hats when they enter a building and women would stop using men's gimmie hats as a fashion statement.

I wish our government would get out of the business of private enterprise and allow those who are willing to sacrifice their blood, sweat, and tears of self-employment to freely operate in a truly free market. I also wish that if the chips fall hard and things just don't work out for them then we, the people, would be allowed to support them by whatever legal means are available and stop the continued waste of taxpayer dollars by the government bailing them out.

I wish cussing were still thought of as being vulgar and the exposure of filthy words that can be seen in public were outlawed.

I wish all tattoos were made with a special ink that faded within one year, and I wish mostly sailors were still the only ones who got tattoos.

I wished we still dressed up for church in dressy clothes, and I wish people would learn the difference between going-to-the-beach clothes and church clothes. While I do enjoy dressing casual for church, there is a big difference between beach casual and dressy casual.

I wish movies were still made for entertainment and not for political statements, and I wish they could be watched with scary parts in them and not vulgar and sadistic scenes. I also wish the love scenes were just kissing scenes that still left room for wonderment.

I wish more people read the word of God for their own personal teachings and not try to decipher some mystical meanings from the scriptures and call them entertainment.

I wish a little bell really would ring every time an angel got their wings. Maybe it would remind all of us what things are really important in this life.

If wishes were dollars, I guess I would be rich.

Old Man Signs

Well, it's now official. I have made a self-determination that I am officially an unofficial old man.

This self-appointed title has been declared by me on myself, so it's my own title that only I can hold. Everyone else is excluded from my title, and my self-made lot in life is not shared with my wife or family.

In other words, I am not really an old man, but I have started doing some old man things. Now some of you are going to disagree with me in my personal observations because you may be young in age and you may find yourself already in my realm of reasoning as to why I have declared myself old.

A few years ago I went into a local restaurant and forced myself to purchase an order of liver and onions. As many of you may remember, eating liver and onions as a young child usually causes crying, gagging, kicking, and screaming fits.

I purchased the order of liver and onions as a personal test to see if my tastes have changed. Surprise! I was able to eat the food at hand, and I can't say I enjoyed it, but I did in fact eat my portion and walked away satisfied. This was my first sign of aging.

My second test came when I entered a seafood house. I have tried many, many different foods in my lifetime. I have eaten alligator, buffalo, coon, armadillo, gar, mountain oysters, but one thing I never enjoyed was raw salt water oysters. Most of us guys have been dared by our dads or teased by our camping buddies about eating raw oysters. As I entered the restaurant, for some reason, out of the blue, I decided it was time to try some raw oysters. I really enjoyed them, and I order them often.

My third test came about two weeks ago. My wife had purchased some buttermilk to try her hand at making buttermilk biscuits equal to her grandmother's biscuits she remembers from years ago. I got up for my morning breakfast, and as I opened the refrigerator I noticed the unopened carton of buttermilk. It caught my eye, and I said to myself I wonder how a glass of buttermilk would taste.

Here again, buttermilk is usually despised by youngsters. Just like the liver and onions, the gag reflex kicks in and once again the crying, kicking, and screaming will start.

I grabbed a glass, poured some of the thick globs of sour milk, drank it down, and lo and behold I really enjoyed it.

My final test came this past weekend. Growing up and working outside most of my early years, I was made to believe that suffering the sweat of pains associated with farming and ranching always made me tough. I watched my dad do mechanic, carpenter, and other outside work. My dad was the kind of guy that if he got a cut, he should simply ignore it, and I never understood how he could handle the pain. I saw him bust his knuckles till they bled, and he seemed to ignore the dripping blood from his hand. He never showed the pain. I tried the same thing as a young man. I never wore gloves. They were for sissies. I never properly protected my eyes while grinding, and protecting my hearing was unheard of. (No pun intended.) Working without a shirt was common, and getting sunburned made my skin leather tough. Going barefoot and walking across stickers with my mulberry-stained feet was the norm. I was tough, at least in my mind. Now I know most of my antics were out-and-out dumb.

I went to the ranch this past weekend and was going to mow the pasture. Normally I would wear a small gimmie hat, and by the end of the day I would be so dirty and sunburned you would think the devil was my half brother. (Okay, a lot of ya'll know my brother, Keith, and I'm not talking about him.)

When I arrived at the ranch this past weekend to crank up the tractor, for some reason my old man's sense caught hold of me. I put on a wide-brimmed hat with a large handkerchief draped over my head and neck before putting on my hat. I placed a breathing mask over my mouth and nose, and I put on a good pair of gloves. After spending eight hours on the tractor in hundred plus degrees, I was hot but protected. I wasn't sunburned, and I could actually breathe without laboring through the dirt and grit that gets in your nose while mowing.

I'm sure as time passes and I get really, really old, more signs shall come to pass that will show my age, but for now I have officially declared myself as the beginnings of an old man. For me, myself, and I, it's a place I really enjoy.

PENCILS

School districts seem to require the students to bring a large amount of pencils and erasers, and it makes me wonder why so many pencils are needed. Well, I think I have the answer.

I'm sure a man created the list. It's very obvious to me the need for such a large number of pencils and erasers. These are two items that carry an extreme need to a grade school boy.

On the very first day of school, most rooms are equipped with brand-new pencil sharpeners. Manual or electric, it is with great necessity and a mark of maturity to be able to go the pencil sharper and sharpen your brand-new pencils. The first one is used for practice. The third and fourth ones are used to simply hear the noise the sharpeners make. As days pass, the pencils and the pencil sharpener are used to get out of schoolwork. It never failed that while the entire class was quiet working on their papers, my pencil point would break, so I naturally had to make my way to the pencil sharpener in the front of the room. Grinding noises during class time was a great distraction. Forcing the handle to turn to the timing of "Jingle Bells" made great laughter in the room. I had great musical talent while sharpening my pencils. Think of the song "Jingle Bells" while you read these words to the rhythm of the song. *Grind, grind, grind. Grind, grind, grind. Grind, grind, grind, grind, grind. Grind, grind, grind. Grind, grind, grind. Grind, grind, grind, grind, grind. Grind, grind, grind.* The tune of "Jingle Bells, jingle all the way." Get it? This musical ability took at least three pencils per day.

The next pencils are used to accidentally drop on the floor during class. By accidentally dropping my pencil eight to ten times, the teacher would call me down, thereby causing my classmates to giggle 'cause I was in trouble again. It also gives all little boys an opportunity to try to look up the little girls' dresses too!

More pencils are needed for the daily sword fights. En guard! Hack, hack, crosscut, crosscut, stab, jab were all part of the day's activities. Many of them were broken. Some were knocked into the commode if we were sword fighting in the restroom during recess. I never did understand why our commode was always stopped up!

Many a pencil has lost its shiny yellow glaze to a manly showing of one's strength. Boys place a pencil with the ring and index finger on top and place their middle finger under the pencil. A swift slap on the edge of the desk or on your leg would break the pencil smooth in half. You just ain't much of a man unless you can break a pencil with one finger. It's also a good way on the first week of school to earn some extra money by betting your friends you can break a pencil with only one finger.

As you get a little older, a sharp number 2 pencil sticks real good into a ceiling tile. When you run out of pencils, the girls always seem to have enough extras.

Some pencils just get chewed up, others legitimacy lost, and some of them actually do the work intended. Some of them are used to play chicken. Palms forward and your friend tries to stab your hand before you move it. Sometimes you win, and sometimes you lose. If you ever want to meet a guy who lost, stop by sometimes. Over fifty years ago, Mike Hennessy beat me in a game of chicken. I wasn't quick enough. I still carry the broken pencil lead tip in my hand to this day.

I haven't even started on the erasers yet, but I sure do hope I have been able to help you understand the need for some many pencils. If you ever need to find out why so many erasers are needed, just ask some of the grade school boys you know. They may have little lumps on their heads. Pencils with a brand-new rubber eraser make good boppers on a guy's head.

Running Off to the Pond

A burr haircut, a pair of underwear (and yes, it was briefs), and some cutoff blue jeans were all the clothes I needed as a kid. My summers were spent outside.

We could wake up in the morning and hit the great outdoors until after dark and never stop. Stopping to eat was a hard thing to do, and we would always put off going to the bathroom till the last moment. Have you ever seen a little kid who is having so much fun they won't stop long enough to go to the bathroom? They wind up crossing their legs and jumping up and down in misery, fearing they may miss a moment's fun.

Summertime for me was a time of great events. First of all, it was the only time we didn't have to get dressed every morning for school. As a boy, I would go around without my shirt because shirts were too cumbersome. I also felt that being without a shirt would toughen my skin, so when I would fight the wild animals around my home like Tarzan did, the scratches wouldn't hurt as much.

Being barefooted made the soles of my feet feel like leather by summer's end, and the old mulberry tree in our yard gave way to permanent die stains on our feet for several weeks. Eventually the sticker burrs that had embedded themselves into our soles would get red and sore so Mama would get out the trusty needle and tweezers.

My dad would use the end of his pocketknife to help us dig stickers, and Mom would always get mad. She always complained about Daddy's pocketknife. He would use it for all sorts of things, from digging stickers out of our feet to cleaning fish, fixing calves, splicing wire, to cutting a slice of cheese. Mama would fuss at him, telling him to get that dirty knife off her food.

"It ain't no tell'n' where you had that thing," she would say.

My feet carried me places I should have never gone. There is a very faint spot in my memory of the time my feet carried me to an old pond way on the backside of our property. Our land was situated on a twelve-acre tract of land. Four acres belonged to my parents, four acres to Aunt Merle, and the other four to Aunt Florence. Aunt Florence's land had an old pond on it.

For whatever reason, I had snuck off from the house and my dog and I went down to this pond. Now before any of you start asking where my mother was in all this, let me make some things perfectly clear.

When I was growing up in Hufsmith, Texas, our road was still a dirt road. Hufsmith Road and Stuebner Airline were both dirt, and the only people who drove down our road were family or very close friends. I can still remember jumping up and running to the window when we heard a car just to see who it was. Times were different then, and when we played outside, the fears and concerns of the safety of the children were lessened by the fewer evils of life at that time.

My mom suddenly heard the dog barking from the opened windows of our unair-conditioned house, and she came out to investigate. To her panic and shock, she found me about a hundred yards away from the house, buck naked, wading in this pond. The dog knew I had gone somewhere I shouldn't have gone, and the dog was in a panic, too, barking and running along the bank of the pond.

When my mama found me, she grabbed up my clothes and me and held me very tight in her arms, hugging me and crying. Then she spanked me and hugged me and cried some more. Then she spanked me and hugged me and cried some more, and as far as I know, I got a small series of hugs and spankings all the way back the house. It has just recently come to my attention that one of the things I did not know at the time was my mom was in the midst of a migraine headache during all this. They used to put her down for several hours at a time, and through all this, she had to go find me way off in the pasture somewhere.

Well, I know several good things came from this story. Number one, I lived to tell about it, and number two, I learned to never go swimming buck naked again. If I had kept my clothes on, the spanking wouldn't have stung so much.

SNAKES AND TURTLES

Wintertime was well on the way. No, not because we had experienced a few days of cool weather, but because the animals were beginning to tell me so.

I was up at the ranch minding my own business when I heard that familiar, strange sound of those cranes flying over migrating toward the south. I figure in a few short weeks I'd have the pleasure of listening to the geese beginning their trek down here too. I enjoying hearing the geese talk to each other.

When I go to the ranch, I climb in my truck and leave town, and for a solid day I don't have to talk to anybody, answer questions for anybody, or even see another human being once I hit our property. Life becomes total silence. If I want to talk, my conversation is always one-sided unless me and the Good Lord are having a heart-to-heart and then sometimes he gives me answers in that still, small voice. Otherwise my bull, cows, or donkeys simply listen without responding. Well, that's not totally true. They do respond, but their response is simply turning tail and walking away.

Another reason I knew winter is on the way is because the snakes were steadily moving. I can't stand snakes. I don't like them, I don't care for them, and the older I get, the more afraid I become of them.

A few weeks earlier, I started hooking up the bucket to my front-end loader on my tractor, and when I lifted the bucket, a long, red snake came rushing out from below its resting place. It scared me to death, and before I could grab anything to hit it with, it rushed away. The next thing I know is, I was minding my own business and noticed movement about ten feet behind me, next to the slab of the garage. I immediately recognized the fact that this was not a friendly kind of snake. It was a water moccasin, and he was looking for cover. I ran to the truck and grabbed my pistol. It was making its way around the corner, still running parallel to the slab of the garage. I knew I could not take a shot from my position because I was facing the garage and that would have meant shooting into a concrete back-stop, so I repositioned myself. Have you ever tried to place a shot with a pistol from ten feet into a one-inch-wide target? It's tough, but I hit the mark. The problem was, however, that the damage I did was not deadly, and he then quickly found a hole in the old wood wall of the garage and climbed inside. I kinda thought he was going to hide between the two walls, but he made his way into the well shed and out of my sight. I was then worried about having this wounded, mad water moccasin running around the place because a water moccasin can become a very, very aggressive snake. They stink too. They give off an odor very similar to a skunk.

I walked through the garage and slowly eased open the door of the well house, and there in the darkened room I saw him lying in the middle of the concrete floor. I had picked up a ten-foot two-by-four and jabbed it into him as hard as I could. Unfortunately, this thing still slithered off and got away from me. Now I'm walking around the garage on egg shells.

Two days later, other family members killed a rattle snake just a few feet away from my first ordeal. Ever since then, I have become more cautious just waiting on our first good freeze to put these guys into their winter slumber.

Another way I know winter is on the way is because the turtles are becoming very aggressive too. My granddaughter and I went fishing last Saturday, and I had placed our catch on a stringer and set them at my feet in the water. After about ten minutes, I decided to check the stringer, and when I pulled the fish out of the water, all I had left were half fish. The turtles had come within three feet of us fishing and methodically began feasting in preparation for their winter's bliss.

The theft of our catch aggravated me, so I set a treble hook on my line and took one of the half-eaten fish and set my line on the bottom. After about three minutes, I saw that long, slow pull on my line, and I knew the turtle had taken the bait. I set the hook and enjoyed the thrill of reeling in a nice-sized turtle. I pulled the turtle out of the water with hook still intact and placed the rod, turtle, and all about ten foot away from the water and grabbed my spare rod. As my granddaughter and I continued fishing, much to our amazement, we suddenly saw the turtle making headways back into the water with rod, reel, line, hook, and sinker all in tow. I jumped and grabbed the rig just as it was entering the water.

To give my granddaughter a fisherman's thrill, I then took the rod and released the drag and let the turtle's head back into open water. After I knew the several yards of line were free, I told her to start reeling him in. It was her first experience of catching something that could really give her a good tug. She loves fishing. Together we fished for almost three hours, and I never heard a complaint.

Yes, wintertime is on the way. The animals have told me so. There was also frost on the roof that morning.

Styrofoam or Styr-Foam
if You're from Texas

"Stupid stuff!"

"I wonder who made up such a stupid idea!"

"I don't know, but look at it. It's only a quarter of an inch thick!"

"It's probably communism. They are trying to make us believe this stuff can really keep things cool."

"Look how light it is. It's just too flimsy."

"What did you say they called it?"

"I think it's called styr-foam."

"Styr-foam, you say? Well, I can guarantee you it'll never make it here in America. It's just too cheap and flimsy."

I can honestly say I remember when Styrofoam was first put on the market. I must have been about six or seven years old when I saw a firsthand experience of this new product.

Along a street in our community, on a road called Zion Road, there stands the old family homestead of Uncle Albert (Big Boy) Hirsch. The same family no longer occupies the house, but the home still stands in a remodeled state.

In the front yard of the home was a large cedar tree that in and of itself carries a story I will share in the future. It was under this tree my story is being told.

Many years ago, my family would hold the Vogt Family Reunion around the Hufsmith, Texas, area. One of the meeting places was Uncle Albert's home.

Some of the men of the families would begin preparing the large barbecue pits on a Saturday night, making them ready for a family feast on Sunday. On Sunday all the family would begin gathering after church to see loved ones they haven't seen for a while and some they have seen too often. You know how family reunions are. The older you get, the more they mean to you, but as a kid, the only reason you went to them is because Mom and Dad made you.

Upon arrival there is always the traditional greeting by all the aunts who wore lipstick. They would pinch your cheeks and plant one on your cheek and you had to run off wiping lipstick. Always the same comments about how much you've grown, how handsome you are, how sweet you appear to be, and all those other stories your aunt can say about you. Once you get there, however, you end up having a good time. Even though all these people are supposed to be your cousins, you can't remember their names from one year to the next.

It's strange how stories can stick in a kid's mind, but I can still see Uncle Albert with a plate of food in his hand. He was looking for a place to sit down and enjoy his meal. Everybody always brought their own drinks to the reunion, and many of you will recall the fact that in the fifties, your standard ice chest was made from metal and not plastic. They always had the built-in bottle opener on one end. They were strong and sturdy.

Uncle Albert saw this white ice chest sitting against the cedar tree, so he decided to rest himself and eat.

As he sat on this particular chest, however, it was made from a new product apparently unknown to him at the time, and of course it was called Styrofoam or styr-foam if you live in Texas.

Whack, bam, boom. The ice chest was obliterated as Uncle Albert fell sideways from the impact of this now crunched clump of plastic under his weight.

I don't remember his exact words when he went down, but I do recall several of the men trying to explain to him about this new invention. Most of their comments were not favorable toward this product, and I think a few of them even predicted its eventual downfall.

I just wish I had purchased stock in the company.

Styr-foam

THE CAKE

Many years ago, I was a member of the Tomball, Texas, Volunteer Fire Department. I am still excited about the fact they trusted me with their equipment. My many calamities of life had not yet occurred, but if they only knew how many boo-boos I had made, they would have likely locked me in the station.

Our group was a close-knit group, as with most groups of this nature. When the chips are down, you have to depend on each other in dangerous times. Volunteer Fire Departments probably serve millions of people across this great nation, and thousands of people volunteer their time to serve the public.

We decided one day to break bread together at someone's home. I don't recall the occasion, but who needs a reason to eat? I am not real sure where the event was held. I simply don't remember.

I decided I wanted to bake a cake for this function, and I was still dating my lovely bride-to-be. I pulled out one of my old cookbooks.

Many, many years ago, my mom bought me a cookbook when I was about ten or eleven years old. I guess it was her first attempt to equality in the kitchen.

I looked through this book properly entitled *My First Cookbook* and found a simple cake made with the basic ingredients. Flour, water, eggs, milk, and several other items, namely, sugar.

I read some terms in the recipe like folding the eggs, blending the mixture, lightly stirring, and of course, being a man, I first laughed at the idea of trying to fold eggs. Can you imagine the mess?

One of the sugar ingredients mentioned was confectioners' sugar, which was to be used for the icing.

I had never heard of this term before. Sugar is sugar. I could discuss pushrods and flywheels, tenpenny nails, nail stretchers, and skyhooks, but I had never heard the term confectioners' sugar.

I made my cake and then set about the process of the icing. I carefully mixed the ingredients and properly measured each item, including the sugar. My sugar was regular sugar, straight from Sugarland, Texas, and I anticipated the end result of laying this luscious cake onto my palate and savoring each sweet taste of this fine creation.

Once the cake was completed, I allowed it to cool, and after a little while, I placed it in my truck and picked up my fiancé.

When she saw the cake, she immediately knew there was a problem and began to expound on the different kinds of sugar and the major difference between confectioners' and granulated sugar.

I took the cake anyway, and we all had a good laugh. I know the cake was eaten, but I heard rumored the local dentist offices were filled the next day with a rush of broken teeth and dentures.

THE CAVE

There is a creek that we played in during my childhood days named Spring Creek. A gully named Bogs Gully intersects with the creek.

The location where the gully meets the creek is called The Bogs Hole. This spot used to be the Sunday afternoon gathering spot in the 1920s, 1930s, and 1940s for the local folk. They could picnic, swim, pitch horseshoes, and the like.

A few yards from this intersection was a spot where people would cross the gully to go a little farther to another location called The Caldwell Hole, named after another family that lived in the woods.

All along the gully, the Mueller boys and I could spend many days of our summers exploring the woods. The Mueller Boys were a family of seven brothers and no sisters. Bobby and Charlie were generally too old for us, middle-aged guys and Tomato Head and Bill Hockey were a little too young to tag along. Most of the time, it was me, VOP, and Rotten Cotton who would make our rounds on the gully and Bimbo would sometimes be there.

The rest of this story begins with a warning. Kids, don't try this! It's very stupid and dangerous!

One day during the 1960s, the Mueller boys got a bright idea about digging a cave in the side of the gully walls. They had started the cave before I saw it, but I was eager to help with the work. In my mind, the cliff was forty or fifty feet high, but I'm sure ten or twelve feet was more like it.

Several days of hard labor had been spent digging this cave, and of course shoring the walls was an unthought-of idea. We were kids, and kids don't think. Especially boys. Boys are indestructible! We never die and never get hurt! That was why shoring the walls or any other safety factor was totally out of the question!

I don't know whose idea it was, but we decided that our digging process was a bit slow. We had already created a good sized area of about four feet by six feet in the side of the wall, but we decided it was time to blast our way a little deeper. We went up to Uncle Johnny's gas station and got several gallons of gasoline in a jug. We felt if we could plant these jugs of gasoline inside our cave, we could create an explosion to loosen the dirt, making the dig much easier. We had these dreams and ideas of a cave large enough to live in if we ever needed to leave home. We saw no need of school and doing chores was the pits, so we figured we could hide away in our new home.

We took these jugs of gas and carefully placed them in the hole. We then saved one jug and backed our way from the entrance pouring gasoline as we moved away anticipating using this trail of gas as our fuse. I don't remember how many jugs of gas we had, but I'm sure it was more than just one. I mean what's the use of only a minor explosion with one jug when three or four would have caused a bigger blast!

As we exited and poured, we soon lit the match and took off running. Down the embankment, through the water-filled gully, and up the other side, we ran with hearts racing in anticipation of a tremendous explosion! We hit the dirt on the other side of the gully and lay behind a log, awaiting the big bang. Ten seconds turned to thirty, and thirty turned to sixty, and one minute turned to two, and soon we wondered what went wrong when a small trickle of black-sooted smoke began to emerge from our cave. Nobody ever told us we had to compress the jugs of gas to make them explode. We had simply put large, open jugs of gas in the hole, and the jugs simply burned like a large coal oil lamp. We waited awhile hoping for an explosion, but it never occurred.

I think that was the last time we ever went down to our cave. It had become black and soot-filled, and occupying the cave any longer was next to impossible.

I think all the Mueller Boys and I ought to get our sons and make a trip down there soon to see if our cave still exists after all these years. I'll just need to remember to carry plenty of soap and water.

The Mueller Boy's and their Mom

THE POT OF BEANS

I enjoy trying to cook. I can cook almost anything that walks, crawls, or flies. I have cooked beef, chicken, fish, crawfish, armadillo, softshell turtle, gar, carp, and a mean pot of beans. Now keep in mind that just 'cause I cooked, it doesn't mean you can eat it. No, sirree, I can botch up the best cut of steak you've ever seen. I can take a steak that costs ten dollars and turn it into a two-bit piece of rubber in a flash.

I've shared stories of my past job at the old Mama Goodson's Cafe in Hufsmith, Texas. They were, and still are, famous for their chicken fried steak. I always watched them beat the steaks on the chopping block, but I never paid attention to the type of batter it is put in before cooking. All I can remember was Ms. Kerri dumping the steaks in something that looked like an egg-and-milk batter, but I never learned the exact sequence of dippings.

I decided one day I was going to cook myself some chicken fried steak while my loving wife was away. (I can't cook when she's at home. She makes me nervous while she's in the kitchen.)

I gathered together the eggs, milk, and flour, as well as a couple of steaks. At first I dipped the steak into the egg, then the milk, and then the flour, back into the egg, into the milk, and back into the flour, but each dunking washed off the first product until I simply had a batch of dripping goo oozing from the steak.

My next batch of batter was the egg, milk, and flour all mixed into one bowl. I dunked the steak into the batter, but I couldn't get the batter to stick to the steaks. It was kinda like the glue we used to make in the first grade from flour and water. It stuck to my hands, the bowl, and to everything else, but it wouldn't adhere to the steak. To solve this problem, I took the steaks in my right hand and attempted to pat this batter on the steak until I had it covered real good, and I eased it into my hot grease.

The steak started to cook real good at first, developing a golden-brown color, so I assumed it was done.

As I removed it from the grease, I placed it on a plate to begin the process of wrapping my lips around this golden-brown creation I had properly named Golden Brown Chicken Fried Steaks by Clifford. As I stabbed the steak with my fork, the fork almost bent in two as the steak slid off on the floor. I had created a rock.

Refusing to admit defeat, I still was chewing on the steak when my wife arrived home.

"How was your supper, honey?" she asked.

"Great," I said as my teeth resisted every chew.

Another favorite food item I enjoy cooking is red beans and rice. I like red beans, but my wife gets on to me when I eat them. I have tried to explain to her that I am doing my part for the environment by creating additional natural gas. I received a gag gift one time that was called Hillbilly Bubble Bath. It was a bag of beans. You cook the beans, eat them, and climb into a tub of soapy water and, well, I guess you get the picture.

Aunt Brenda saw me cook my beans one time, and she wouldn't eat them. I simply tore open the package and poured the bag into the pot. She informed me right away that beans sometimes contain small stones in the bag. I didn't know this, and she refused my beans, and I have since learned to wash and separate the beans before cooking.

The only time I am now allowed to cook is at the ranch, usually during deer season. One day several years ago, I started an early morning pot of beans. As my pot of beans were cooking, they began to develop that natural roll of boiling in the water. You've seen it before. A pot full of beans can roll over and over inside the pot. As my beans began this roll, a friend of the family's named Albert Sebach walked over to the pot to see what I was cooking.

Albert was a bachelor. Albert had his own way of doing things. His way was the only way, but he would never interfere even though he always thought your way was the wrong way. His personal and people skills were part of the exclusive bachelor club variety. Albert had a bad habit of cussing a lot, so when he began to cuss my beans, it really didn't bother me too much, but in between the bad language and body language of discontent, I was able to decipher his main question of "What in the blankety-blank world are you cooking in this pot?" As I walked over to the pot, I saw with amazement a large glob of something in the pot of beans.

I grabbed the nearest spoon, and as I dug this glob of yuk from the pot, I came to realize the pot holder had been accidentally deposited into the pot of beans. The best I can surmise was when I took the lid off during cooking, I must have laid the lid on top of the pot holder. The condensation from the boiling water on the lid had caused the pot holder to attach itself to the lid, and the rest is history.

I have to admit, however, we were extremely hungry, and the rice, cornbread, and red beans were sure good eatin'!

THE THINKER

Delicate matters require delicate storytelling. This is one of those matters, and you will need to read between the lines. I would like to say this story is for men only, but I know that would simply make women want to read it, but all in all most women will probably not find this story funny. On the other side of the fence, however, most men will probably recall similar events in their own life and begin laughing their head off at an issue that occurred to me many years ago.

I need to plant an image in your mind. *The Thinker.* Do you know what *the Thinker* is? It is a statue located somewhere in the world made by somebody who I don't know that shows a man in a sitting position with his elbow on his knee and his hand made into a fist placed firmly under his chin. It gives you a symbol of someone deep in thought. It is also a position many men have found themselves in while sitting at certain times on certain items in certain rooms.

Years ago my family went on a short two-day trip to East Texas, and we stopped at a large, very nice convenience store in Madisonville called Buc-ees'. It was my first time to ever enter one of these establishments, and I must say the place was impressive. The facilities were clean, and the store is first class. Inside the men's room is a wall of stalls that has a half door to each separate resting area. The doors have a lock on them that when locked from the inside, they reflect a sign outside the door that shows vacant or occupied.

As I surveyed each door for a vacant sign, I soon found one and grabbed the handle and pulled the door toward me as they all swung outward. When I opened the door, I was startled by a man who was seated in the thinking position, but in this case he had both hands under his chin and his head was bowed downward with his boxers below his knees and his pants on the floor. As soon as I opened the door, I was taken aback and immediately tried to close the door and this man did not flinch. I mumbled a pitiful "excuse me" in his direction as I attempted to reshut the door. The door was about two-thirds open.

I did my best to close the door with my left hand, but the door seemed extra heavy, and I was very definitely in an awkward position because of course there I was standing right in front of this guy, but he never moved. This moment was very embarrassing to me, but at the same time this guy acted like he never even heard me. Once again in a split second, I tried to close the door and once again it would not budge. I quickly stepped behind the door to remove him from my view, and I then took both hands and placed them on the door and once again gave it a semihard push, but it still would not budge.

Now you have to keep in mind, all this was split-second decisions, but then I thought maybe the door had a door closure on it that had jammed, so I stuck my head back around the end of the door to check for it closer, and as I did, I then realized how perverted this looked, but the guy had still not moved a twitch. He was in the same position. I quickly surveyed the top of the door and did not locate a closer and once again repositioned myself behind the door and out of his and my view from each other. This time I leaned onto the door with my shoulder, thinking the hinges were jammed and still no movement. All I got was just a spongy bounce back of the door as I hit it again with my shoulder hoping to break it loose so it would close.

As I turned my head for a final shoulder punch like a football block, I noticed a couple of guys standing away from me were already beginning to grin at the whole scene being played out in front of them. I, too, was about to start laughing, and as I hit the door again. Still the door wouldn't budge when I noticed neatly tucked between the edge of the door and the door jamb and hinges the man's walking cane that had fell in the crack and was blocking the door's closure. By then I was totally embarrassed and actually wondered if I had broken this guy's cane. I quickly exited the facilities with two guys laughing and me trying to get out of there as fast as possible. There was no way that I was going to go back around the end of the door and ask this gentleman to remove his cane. As I threw my head back for one last look to see if he had moved, and there he was, in the same position and just thinking.

UNCLE SPEEDY

"Clifford, come here!"
"Clifford, can you hear me, boy, I said get in here!"

"Sir," I said as I entered the unfinished kitchen.

"Look at this. Every one of these styles are a sixty-fourth too short or long."

"What's a style, Uncle Speedy, and how short did you say they were?"

"I said they were each a sixty-fourth too short or too long, and a style is the divide between each door on these cabinets!"

"Okay, but Uncle Speedy, what's a sixty-fourth?" I asked.

"Clifford, how long have you been working on cabinets?"

"Well, Uncle Speedy, I've only done this a couple of times before, but I still don't understand what a sixty-fourth is!"

"Come here and look at this ruler. Do you see each of these little marks between the inch marks? That's a sixty-fourth!"

"Do you mean those little, bitsy, teeny, tiny marks?"

"Yes, Clifford, each one of those marks represent one sixty-fourth of an inch!"

"But, Uncle Speedy, what difference does one sixty-fourth make? I can't even see it, much less cut it any closer!"

"Look at it this way, Clifford. If you had a cabinet sixty-four feet long and you cut every style one sixty-fourth shorter than the one before, how short would the cabinets be at the end?"

Now even though I had to go through Mrs. Beard's remedial math course three times to get through high school, I was still able to calculate the answer when I finally confessed to him it would be an inch out of whack. That's a lot when you're working on cabinets, and they hadn't invented one-inch caulk yet.

This was one of my first lessons in cabinetmaking from Uncle Speedy Bogs. Now Uncle Speedy really wasn't my uncle, but because all The Mueller Boys called him Uncle Speedy, I called him Uncle Speedy too.

I had often asked my dad how Speedy got his name. He confessed to me that it was a nickname given him by all his boyhood friends. He had one crippled foot, and they always had to wait on him when they were running anywhere, so they just nicknamed him Speedy. The name stuck even in light of its original, cruel connotation. We men are like that, you know. We take the worst things about a guy and poke fun at them, and as we get older, we soon realize the nickname given each one of us is really a true bonding of friendship. Many men carry nicknames from childhood. Moose, Goose, Unk, Speedy, Shorty, Fat Albert, Dog, Bimbo, Cotton, Squirrel, Hoss, Peg, Runt, Blackie, Whitie, Stick, Stinky, Blue, Suds, Shine, Hair, Monkey, Smitty, and Popeye are just a few of the nicknames that have stuck with men for their entire lives. When the name is first anointed on them, it is usually at a young age. It is initially intended to poke fun at each other, but as we grow older, we soon realize the name is no longer intended in harming or poking fun at you, it's simply a way of being accepted by other men with common problems, likes, and ideas. I don't expect my female readers to understand the bonding two men have when their nickname is used as an everyday, common expression of friendship and acknowledgement.

Uncle Speedy was the older of two brothers in the Bogs family. Uncle Speedy's brother was named Dan. Their mom and dad were known to me as Uncle Johnny (whom we boys later nicknamed Blister Butt and that's another whole story) and Aunt Eunice Bogs. Mary Louise was their sister. Uncle Speedy was a little older than my dad was, and they had some good times together.

Late in life, Uncle Speedy met a lady named Shirley, and with her, she brought an instant family to Uncle Speedy. One girl and three boys: Angel, Kyle, Eddie, and Randy.

Now if the truth were told, I could remember plenty of times Uncle Speedy had to holler at the boys while on the jobsite. However, he wasn't always hollering because he was mad. He usually hollered because, as with most young men, we are thickheaded and have a one-track mind, and hollering is the only thing the boys and I usually paid attention too.

It takes a good man to open his heart to a woman, and it takes an extra good woman to open her heart to a man. We men tend to need more and more care by our spouses as we get older because God has placed nature in such an order that we usually pass from this life first. It takes a great man to open his heart, his home, and his wallet to children, as was the case with Uncle Speedy. To fall in love with a woman is normal, but to also fall in love with her children from another marriage takes a special person, and Uncle Speedy filled the shoes real well.

Uncle Speedy passed away many years ago, and as I made my way to the funeral home, I began to realize more and more the men in my life are slowly leaving this earth, creating a void in my heart. I began to think about my dad and the people from Hufsmith and the kids who played on the same ground before me as I was able to play on. I realized my own son has walked some of the same soil as my dad and Uncle Speedy and many of the other kids from Hufsmith have.

My heart was heavy, but my spirits held high, as I know Uncle Speedy is probably playing Kick the Can with my dad somewhere in heaven's yard.

WATER AND GAS

I have always volunteered to help anybody I can with small handyman projects, but over the years, even some preachers have asked me to stay away from workday around the church house. I have been replaced.

My wife and I started our home in a small honeymoon cottage in Montgomery County, Texas. The home was located on Hufsmith Dobbin Road. It was a one-bedroom with one bath, a kitchen, and a small living room. Eighty-two dollars a week was my income, and we went out to eat every weekend and still had money left over.

Our first home purchase was a mobile home located on a small plot of land purchased from Uncle Johnny Bogs in Hufsmith, Texas. In time we sold the mobile home and moved to a small two-bedroom frame home on the property. The house still stands in front of a local café named Mel's.

The home was built in the forties and was good quality. After the movers moved the home to the property, they leveled it and did a few Sheetrock repairs, but connecting the home to various utilities was left in my hands. We had a septic tank, public water, butane, and of course electricity.

Men learn by experience, but a real man never admits to his wife his lack of knowledge in various areas. To do so would make us vulnerable to weakness, so we tend to overstate our qualifications. One experience will give us knowledge in certain areas and the second time around we learn a little more and the third time a little more and so on and so on and so on.

I've tried to repair a lot of things I knew absolutely nothing about, but after tearing the thing open, I learned something new and my experience with my new home taught me well.

The first two items I hooked up were the sewer and electricity. I then moved on to the water, and I was saving the gas for last.

Homes in those days were piped with half inch galvanized pipe for both water and gas. I dug the ditch and got my tools together after laying the new line, and I proceeded to connect the first pipe to the water line. After about a half day's work, I was pleased. It was now time to turn the water on and fresh flowing water would soon be running freely in my new home.

I turned the water on and proceeded from the meter in the yard to inside the house to bleed the air from the faucets, hoping to hear that belch of air clean the pipes and see fresh, clean water burst from each faucet in the home.

As I made my way into the front door, I went to the kitchen and turned the faucet on only to find no pressure at all. I then proceeded to the bathroom and found the same thing—no water. My ear suddenly picked up on the refreshing sound of running water, and I ran back into the kitchen, but no water was running from the faucet, but I heard a distinct sound of running water. I then walked back outside and around the home thinking maybe an outside faucet was running, but I found none. I then made a path through the kitchen, into the bathroom, and out the front door checking all faucets but saw absolutely no running water.

I then lay on the ground peering under the home only to see water beginning to run out the base of the floor onto the ground. A busted pipe inside the wall was my first reaction. I then ran back inside the home and checked all pipes under and behind the sinks, tub, and commode but saw no running water??????

As I made my way back into the kitchen, I happened by the gas stove…, It was so cute. The burners on a gas stove look like those water fountains in a park when they are pumping water!!!!!

WHY ME, LORD?

I f I were ever to write a prayer, it would probably go something like this. Why me, Lord? Why is it that when I go to a department store, the person in front of me has selected an item that won't scan properly and a price check has to be done? Why me, Lord? Why is it that when I buy something at a store, the tag for scanning is always wrong or has completely been rubbed off? Why me, Lord? Why is it that when I go fishing, it rains, or better yet, why is it that I go fishing at the same exact spot where somebody told me to go and I can't catch a thing when they have claimed they just left that spot less than an hour ago and they mopped up on fish? Why me, Lord? Why is it that when I go to the cabinet to retrieve a towel to dry off on, it just so happens that I grab the one and only, flimsiest, scrawny, no-dry-off kind of towel? Why me, Lord? Why is it that when I climb into my wife's car, it's always on empty? Why me, Lord? Why is it that every time I open the refrigerator, I can't find anything? I complain to my wife and she walks right up to the fridge and there it is sitting right in front of my eyes. Why me, Lord? Why is it that every time I go to the restroom, the toilet paper is out and the extra roll is always in the other bathroom? Why me, Lord? Why is it that every time I have a chance to sleep late, I wake up early, or if I need to get up early, I sleep late? Why me, Lord? Why is it that when I have a bad taste in my mouth, I spit out my truck window, and it hits the side of my truck right after I just washed it? Why me, Lord? Why is it that when the bar soap I have in my shower finally breaks in two because it has gotten so small, the only extra bar of soap in the house for showering is a bar of Lava? Why me, Lord? Why is it that when I need to lose weight, I'm hungry, and when my weight issue is okay, I'm not hungry anymore? Why me, Lord? Why is it that if I need to be someplace and I leave early to beat the traffic, the traffic is light, but if I get started a little late, the traffic is real heavy? Why me, Lord? Why is it that when I go to the movie and get in the shortest line, it takes the longest time to get waited on? Why me, Lord? Why is it that when I ask a sales clerk for help, they have on one of those tags that shows they are in training and they don't know the store any better than I do? Why me, Lord? Why is it that I can change the batteries in all my flashlights in the house, and the next time I need one, the batteries have already drained down from age? Why me, Lord? Why is it that when I was a young teenager I thought my parents were dumb, and when my kids were teenagers, they thought I was dumb too? Why me, Lord? Why is it that when cattle prices are low, we have a drought and need to sell, but when cattle prices are real high, we have plenty of grass? Why me, Lord? Why is it that fire ants build their nest in the yard but don't build them in the road ditches? Why me, Lord? Why is it that when a construction job is bid at a certain price you always miss some cost and the profits are low, but when you bid a job cost plus the job cost are even lower and you make less money? Why me, Lord? Why do cows always get out of the pasture on the coldest night of the year when the moon is at its darkest and your day at work was a real pain? Why me, Lord? Why does the price of land go down the moment I make an investment? Why me, Lord? Why can I go to a hardware store and buy two of everything I need to repair my project only to forget the main thing I went in the store for in the first place, or better yet why do the parts I require always need special order?

Life has a lot more "why mes," but you know what? I'm glad to be able to complain about things that really have no importance in life. It means my life is really good, and for that I thank God.

About the Author

A burr haircut, cutoff pants, barefoot, and no shirt was a typical summer day in the life of the younger Clifford. It was a time when a stick became a sword to chop up the monsters or cut down a tree like Paul Bunyan. A really good stick could mow down Grandma's Elephant Ear plants or create a pathway through the pasture. It was a time before families had two cars and mothers didn't run the kids all over the country to visit friends. Any friends you had typically lived the next pasture over. He had to walk to their house or arrange a preplanned meeting the day before from the confines of his secret, boys-only, no-girls-allowed clubhouse in the woods.

In time his territory expanded with a self-repaired bicycle. He soon added a Briggs and Stratton lawn mower motor to his bicycle or some other wheeled contraption.

Clifford's high school years were spent in FFA or shop classes with little to no interest in real book learnin'. His classroom time was spent making animal noises from the back of the room to aggravate his teachers. He calculated that he could make more money if he was outside working instead of sitting in a classroom trying to understand some novel named *Les Miserables*.

He has been told he could run for public office without a hitch. Anything he has done in life that may be bad has already written about by himself. Stories contain such antics such as while being selected to be an altar boy in his local church, he and his buddies would eat the communion wafers, or to the story about swiping a box of ladies' products just to see what they looked like.

As an adult, Clifford succeeded in life through various self-employed business ventures, and all along the way, he has held onto his boyhood antics through pranks, jokes, and overall bullcorn while building a wonderful family and spreading a lot of happiness to others through his true life stories.

CPSIA information can be obtained
at www.ICGtesting.com
Printed in the USA
BVHW071456141019
561050BV00003B/234/P